CUCINA SIMPATICA

CUCINA SIMPATICA

ROBUST TRATTORIA COOKING

JOHANNE KILLEEN & GEORGE GERMON

PHOTOGRAPHS BY KEN AMBROSE

HarperCollins*Publishers*

FIRST EDITION

Designed by Paul and Dolores Gamarello / Eyetooth Design Inc.

Library of Congress Cataloging-in-Publication Data

Killeen, Johanne, 1949–
    Cucina simpatica : robust trattoria cooking / by Johanne
Killeen and George Germon. — 1st ed.
        p.   cm.
    Includes index.
    ISBN 0-06-016119-1
    1. Cookery, Italian.   2. Al Forno (Restaurant :
Providence, R.I.)
I. Germon, George, 1945– .   II. Title.
TX723.K47   1991   90-55816
641.5945—dc20

91 92 93 94 95 CG/RD 10 9 8 7 6 5 4 3 2 1

For Bunny

CONTENTS

ACKNOWLEDGMENTS

To the heroes, the people who have helped us build and maintain our restaurants. They thoroughly understand the need to open the doors each day and to that end they have never failed us: Steve Sevigny and his crew Kevin, Chris, Matt, and Greg; Hugh Vaughan; Don Brown and his sons; Frank Simas and his assistant Joe; Larry Giorgi, senior and junior; Martin and Betty Ann Israelit; South Attleboro Welding; Heffernan Riggers; Arthur Bergel; Butch Klang; and John Loria.

In addition, special thanks to: Ken Hunnibell; our patient partners, Tom Bates and Joshua Miller, at Lucky's and The Hot Club; our loyal staff, past and present, especially Karen Densmore, Pumpkin Vanderpoel, Nancy Miller, Lucia O'Reilly, Marie Owen, Jim Ridgely, and Vinny Scotto; and more than ten years of wonderful customers, without whom we could never have come this far.

Specifically, for this book, we would like to acknowledge: Judith Weber, Richard Sax, Kitty Florey, Max Loubiere, and Michael McLaughlin for their help and inspiration; Lisa Ekus for everything; and finally, Susan Friedland, who shaped our words into a book, spread her enthusiasm throughout HarperCollins, and worked tirelessly to make this happen.

INTRODUCTION

When we try to explain to people why we made the move from the visual arts to the art of cooking, we have a difficult time because the transition seems so natural to us, so logical. For us, our restaurant, Al Forno, is simply an art project that keeps evolving. The kitchen is our studio, and the food we cook is like a canvas that is continually being repainted, changed, and refined. Food is eaten the way art is perceived; it is digested and recorded. Given the right circumstances, a connection is made and communication takes place, which is what art is all about.

Both of us were trained as artists—Johanne as a photographer at the Rhode Island School of Design (RISD), George as a sculptor and potter at the Massachusetts College of Art and later at RISD, where he also taught—and when we decided to open a restaurant, the idea was greeted with incomprehension by a lot of our friends. I think people believed we were giving up art for some lesser, more trivial pursuit—that we were denying our backgrounds and our talents, abandoning art by channeling our energies into something as banal and evanescent as feeding people.

But we've always seen cooking as closely related to the other arts. Life, ideally, is a seamless weaving together of all its elements; it's the whole package. Many great artists knew this—Monet at Giverny, Picasso, Calder. It doesn't make sense to try to paint well, or make beautiful music, or do whatever it is that you do as perfectly as you can, and then not eat the best possible food as well. The unique sensual and tactile pleasures offered by food and eating are among life's greatest pleasures.

We think of cooking as a change of medium. Through cooking we want to influence people, to trigger recollections and associations, to conjure up feelings, and in the process to create a world. We make art that's ephemeral, art that disappears—but so do actors and dancers and musicians. Like them, we hope its impact will linger. We want the little universe we've created, made up of smells and tastes and memories, to reverberate in people's lives long after the meal is eaten.

Johanne and George assemble with the staff of Al Forno for a meal of (clockwise): Grilled Onion Salad with Shaved Parmigiano (page 52); Charred and Peeled Bell Peppers (page 150); and Spaghettini with Watercress Aglio-Olio (page 113).

We want people to take the same joy in sharing food that we do. We wish everyone who loves food could come to Al Forno to participate in it with us. But since Providence, Rhode Island, is a long way from most places, we've written this cookbook.

You may wonder what kind of backgrounds a couple of fanatically dedicated visual-artists-turned-cooks come from. The interesting thing about our origins is how perfectly they work together in terms of the food we create. One reason it's so much fun for us to cook together is the way our ideas bounce back and forth, as Johanne's heritage and life experiences reinforce George's and vice versa. We've both often said that we'd never want to run a restaurant alone. We cook to please each other; the give-and-take, the exchange of ideas and of constructive criticism, the merging of our sensibilities and attitudes—all this is a big part of the pleasure we take in going to work each day.

In a mysterious way, we're all enormously influenced by our childhood experiences. The smallest thing—a brief experience, a person on the periphery of our life, a chance encounter with something new and strange—can leave profound marks on us. When Johanne was a child, for example, she accompanied her mother, a physician, on house calls in her neighborhood. She remembers going to Italian households and sitting there in somebody's living room, waiting for her mother, while the smells of the family's dinner cooking wafted out to her from the kitchen, and developing a bad case of what she calls "Italian envy." All that good olive oil, and sausage, and herbs—those early memories put a strong and permanent stamp on Johanne's approach to food.

George knows that one of his formative experiences as a cook and, probably, as a person, can also be traced back to a visit to the home of a neighborhood family. They were Russian and Czechoslovakian— very different from his Greek-Italian family—and they invited him over one Halloween night to have supper with them. He was eight or nine, but he has never forgotten the smell that hit him when he walked through their front door. It was the smell of a wood fire; the family was gathered around the fireplace grilling meat on skewers that the father had made out of twigs from the yard. There were cider and doughnuts, too, and probably other good things, but the smell of the fire and the meat, and that communal gathering around the hearth, have stayed with George vividly all these years. He remembers thinking, *This is it, this is the way to live.*

George's family didn't cook in the fireplace—his mother was horrified when he came home from his neighbors' house with that idea!—but looking back on it now he sees how extraordinary his family meals were. Both parents could cook, and cook well, but his father was the head chef, and the food he produced on a daily basis was amazing. Frozen or canned vegetables were never served; everything was fresh each day from the market, and all of it was plain and simple and fabulous: just meat and vegetables, fish or chicken and a salad—whatever was available that looked good, but always perfectly cooked.

George learned a lot from his parents, and when he left home he fell into situations where he kept learning—often in places where you wouldn't expect to come into contact with good cooking. For instance, he once had a gas-station job tuning motorcycle exhausts, where he worked with a Cuban fellow who cooked lunches on the kerosene stove in the station. He'd make rice-and-bean dishes with a little beef or chicken, and he always had a pocketful of spices in a little envelope that his wife packed for him to take to work each morning. He taught George a lot, and so did the artist he once worked for as a production potter. They cooked Mexican food for lunch—great stuff—and what kept George sane while he sat at the wheel and threw perhaps three or four hundred casseroles a day was imagining what he'd cook in all those pots if he had the chance.

A few years later, George had the good fortune to work for a chef from Barbados, a so-called black-hat chef: an honorary title reserved for those who cook for British royalty. Whitney was a tremendous influence on George. West Indian, Cuban, and Mexican cooking—all of these cuisines are part of what we bring into the kitchen every day.

Johanne's background is less quirky than George's, a little more sophisticated. George had never tasted quiche, for example, until one of our recent trips to France. He had to ask Johanne what it was, and she couldn't believe it. "How did you miss the great American quiche explosion?" she asked, and all George could say was that he was probably cooking black beans and rice on a kerosene stove in a gas station at the time.

Johanne comes from an extraordinary family. Her mother was widowed early and was left with two small daughters to support; she also had a busy medical practice. She was a woman who loved food but had very little time for it—the kind of frustrated food lover who subscribes to *Gourmet* magazine but has to be satisfied with reading it on the run and fantasizing about great meals. Most of the household cooking was done by a Polish aunt who, when she let herself go, produced some wonderful food, but the usual daily dinner was standard fifties' fare.

Holidays, though, were special. Johanne's mother got to indulge herself; she'd dig out the stack of old *Gourmet*s, plan for weeks, and prepare for days. At Christmastime, Aunt Sophie made her legendary butter cookies and Polish pirogis, and various other family members produced their specialties. Johanne has fond memories of wonderful pastries made by a talented cousin with a part-time job in a bakery. The kitchen would be a happy madhouse, full of aunts and uncles and cousins. There would often be thirty relatives at Christmas dinner, seated at tables all over the house. Johanne gets a little misty-eyed describing it; there was a ceremonial quality to those joyful holiday feasts that she has never forgotten and that is a big part of her attitude toward food to this day—the idea that food is celebration, something you prepare with passion and care and then sit down to with people you love.

Johanne discovered a whole new angle on food when she went to Italy after college to continue her study of photography. In spite of her family's fabulous holiday dinners, her aunt's Polish cooking, several childhood trips to Europe, and an early introduction to the restaurants of Manhattan, Johanne always says that she never really knew what food was until that year in Italy when she ate in the trattorias of Florence and the nearby towns. It was as if she were eating for the first time, and it changed her life.

After returning from Italy, Johanne started her own photography business in Providence, and she used to get into serious cooking in her little apartment kitchen as a break from working in the darkroom.

When she reached the point where she couldn't stand darkness and solitude anymore, she'd emerge into the kitchen, into the air and the light, get out her old *New York Times International Cookbook,* and whip up something wonderful for friends—improvising, cooking from her memories of Italy, putting her own stamp on the food to please the people she was close to, and learning by doing.

Johanne eventually got into food on a professional basis by sheer necessity: She overextended herself on a Hasselblad camera and had to make some money fast, so she took a job in a sort of glorified sandwich shop in Providence. The fellow who ran the place could see that Johanne was gifted, and he offered her the challenge of developing the dessert line for a more ambitious restaurant he planned to open.

At the time, George had been involved not only in his own art (pottery that gradually evolved into sculpture) and in teaching, but in building—something that has fascinated him since he learned the basics of the building trades as a boy from his uncles. Johanne's boss, Dewey, was a friend of George's who hired him to build his new restaurant and then to be chef there. We had been acquainted slightly at RISD, but it was in the kitchen at Dewey's restaurant that we really got to know each other. I suppose you could say that we fell in love over the stove, with cooking aromas wafting around us. For us, kitchens have always been very romantic places.

It was a long road from there to opening our own restaurant, but it always seemed to us like an inevitable step, one that we worked toward for years. The first Al Forno served only breakfast and lunch. We remodeled the entire place ourselves, designing the space, engineering the equipment, and working hard at building both the restaurant and our relationship. After a series of delays both comical and disastrous, we finally opened. We'd get there at 5 A.M. and start making breakfast: little fruit tarts and beignets we developed that were similar to the ones served at the Cafe du Monde in New Orleans, except that ours were baked right on the stone floor of the oven. The lunch menu was equally simple, but there were just the two of us, the work was intense, and we never got home until one in the morning. It didn't take long for us to realize that we loved it and that we were doing the right thing, even though we weren't making a dime. One of the many wonderful customers we've become friendly with over the years wrote a poem to our breakfast place that included the line

> *Quiet and quality here impart*
> *A kindly sense of living art.*

That sums up a lot of what we were trying to do: provide plain, well-prepared food in an oasis of serenity and good will. Our philosophy hasn't changed over the years.

Gradually, we added dinners and eliminated breakfasts and lunches, and the restaurant blossomed. A couple of years ago we opened a second restaurant, Lucky's, and then relocated Al Forno upstairs in the same building.

The restaurants are similar in terms of our standards for the food, but there are important differences. Lucky's can be described as French, specifically Provençal, but it expands to include all of the elements that have gone into French cuisine, including Moroccan and Vietnamese. Al Forno is more purely Italian. Our love affair with Italy never diminished, but the Italian cooking we do is eclectic, always changing, always open to new influences as we taste and read and travel and experiment. The recipes in this book reflect the cooking at Al Forno. Lucky's is another story and maybe, someday, another book.

The recipes we present here have evolved over the years through a great deal of thought and conversation and long, happy hours at the stove. One of the big influences on our cooking has been our travels through Italy and France. What we most like to do in our scarce leisure time is travel, and what we like to do when we travel is eat and walk. We plan our trips abroad not around museums or monuments but around restaurants. We eat lunch and immediately start thinking about where to have dinner, and after dinner there's tomorrow's lunch to consider . . .

In between meals, we take long walks through whatever city or village we happen to be in, looking at the architecture, watching the people—and checking out the restaurants. The walking keeps us fit;

that's important when you have as much contact with food as we do. But what's much more valuable is the richness of what we see, the sights and smells, and the indefinable nuances of other cultures. We're like sponges: We can't see enough or taste enough. We cram every day full, and everything has its effect. We both also have good taste memories: We can analyze a dish and then reproduce it later, at home. When we return from France or Italy, we're always tremendously excited and can't wait to get into the kitchen and work with what we've learned.

Much of the food we serve and many of the recipes in this book involve grilling, and while most of the cooking we do is collaborative, George is responsible for the predominance of grilled food in our repertoire. Johanne often kids George about his passion for making fires and cooking food on them. George can't walk down a beach without looking for driftwood and a sheltered spot to make a fire, and one of his greatest pleasures has been engineering the ovens and hearths we use in our restaurants, with their complex flues and vents and cooking surfaces.

For both of us, the allure of grilling food revolves around the romance of the fire and the irresistible appeal of the aromas and flavors of foods cooked over it. We're drawn into the warmth and ceremony of it as well as the element of mystery. The range of tastes different woods impart to food is vast. We fire our grills at the restaurant with hardwood charcoal. Then we add small pieces of aromatic wood at the edge of the fire where it smolders, and its smoke curls lazily around the food above it, imparting its subtle flavor. We love the sweet smoke of applewood, the spicy smoke from grapevines from Sakonnet Vineyards, or the unmistakable perfume from lilac branches. Each is different and wonderful.

The first time we traveled to Tuscany together, George was fascinated by the raised-hearth fireplaces in the trattorias. The fire would be made from grapevines, twigs, and various small pieces of wood. A square grill with legs and a handle would be placed over it, and the food cooked fast and to order. George was enchanted. The smell of olive oil dripping onto hot embers, the taste of the food with the subtle hint of smoke clinging to it, that little bit of char, the crisp outside of the meat or vegetable, and the seared-in tenderness of the inside—he was drawn in by all the elements. He said to himself: *We have to do that*—and grilling always been an important part of all our operations ever since.

George jokes that real men like to grill: It's fun, and there are no pots and pans and very little cleanup. Men walk away from the grill heros. Grilling is neither difficult nor complicated. You can use an outdoor kettle-type barbecue grill, a hibachi, or your living-room fireplace. We do a lot of grilling at home. It's easy to build up a primitive hearth with bricks and a grill—you can make it as low or as high as you need, and it's endlessly adjustable. Like any new project, it takes some practice to get the results exactly right. The taste of smoke should never overpower the taste of the food, and the perfect combination can be achieved only by trial and error. But you should get the hang of it quickly. It is, after all, an ancient method of cooking, a tried-and-true technique in many cultures, and we urge you to jump in and try it. We think the results will delight you.

If grilling is George's particular passion, then desserts are Johanne's. At Al Forno, we make each dessert individually, to order. We have this down to a science, with tart dough ready to be formed and filled with fresh fruit, a dozen tiny ice-cream makers ready to leap into action, and a selection of cookie doughs ready to be baked. George feels that the desserts may be the strongest part of the menu and one of the elements that sets us apart from other restaurants. Some of our desserts are elaborate, filling, and beautiful to look at, while others are light and simple.

Our grilled foods, our desserts, all our cooking is influenced by our travels. The more we travel, the more we experience and think about what we do, and the freer we become to experiment and innovate, and reach back into our lives to find what pleases us. George has always enjoyed the way a little bit of sweetness combines with various foods. Through research, we have discovered that many cultures cook with a sweet element contrasted by something sour or spicy. In Italian, *agrodolce* means "sweet and sour," and there are several classic examples of this type of cooking in Italian cuisine. This is the inspiration for our Grilled Caponata, for example, for such chutney recipes as Honeyed Onions, and for our Spicy Tomato Catsup, which is begun by caramelizing sugar. We've learned that caramelizing sugar actually removes the sweetness, and that what it adds to, say, a chutney or a savory dish is a richness and depth you can't figure out—a bit of a surprise. And yet this style of sweet-and-sour cooking is perfectly traditional, a classic element in the cuisines of many countries.

Our travels influence not only our cooking but the ambience of our restaurants. We like the scale of European restaurant interiors—they tend to be smaller, lower, and more intimate than their American counterparts—so at Al Forno we lowered the height of our chairs and tables to create this feeling. We put a lot of thought into figuring out the most efficient layout for the kitchen, into devising floor plans and choosing colors, into the whole complex of sensations that make up the restaurant environment—not just those that are immediately connected to the food, such as the smell of meat grilling on an applewood fire as you pull into the parking lot, but the more subtle elements of architecture and design: the quality of the light as it's reflected off a charcoal-gray wall, or the way the placement of the tables relates to the window recesses.

The visual aspect of our restaurants is vital to their success—as is the way the food looks, which is all tied up with the way it smells and tastes. This doesn't mean we're fans of fussy presentation; we like a plate to look artistic but not finicky or full of inedible extras. Everything on a plate has to be an integral part of the dish and contribute to the complexity of flavors.

This visual component of food is individual to every cook—and so, in the end, is the taste of the food. A recipe is a starting point, a way of approaching food, a possibility, rather than a blueprint for a work of art etched in stone. It's important to experiment with taste and smell, to work your way through a concept. A good cook uses a recipe, or the memory of a wonderful meal, as a reference point, just as a carpenter uses one wall in a building as a starting point from which to take measurements. Everything continually goes back to that original reference, so you can see where you come from and where you're headed. But the individual tastes and attitudes and the background of the artist, the carpenter, the cook, are always there, always part of the interpretation.

This doesn't mean that these recipes can't be followed exactly as written. But like all good recipes, they can also be used as tools for learning, as inspiration. They can evolve along with the cook in a way that's infinitely exciting. Cooking isn't casual, but you can become casual about it once you do something enough times that it becomes second nature to you. Until methods of cooking that work for you are an integral part of your life in the kitchen, you might want to follow recipes precisely.

How do you inspire people not to be afraid of cooking? It helps to understand what you're doing, and we try to supply that basic understanding in our recipes. A cook who works in the kitchen without comprehension is merely a good technician, but if everything falls into place and makes sense, then you've taken the first step toward being a truly inspired cook. Care and attention and an unswerving interest in what you're doing go a long way. We believe that if you start with an open mind, and with complete honesty about what you know and what you don't know, you will soon be able to trust your own judgment.

The maddening, challenging, endlessly interesting thing about food as a medium is that it's never predictable. By its nature it's perishable, pathetically dependent on the weather, and subject to the vagaries of the various transportation systems that move it from origin to market. You always have to work with what you've got—what's available on any given day. It's probably been said in every cookbook ever written that the quality of the ingredients you use is vital to the success of a dish—and that's absolutely true. We don't include in our recipes any ingredients that can't be found in the average American supermarket (with a few exceptions that require a trip to the local Italian specialty shop). If an ingredient might be problematic, we try to suggest an alternative or a source. But every once in a while an ingredient is simply unavailable, or of poor quality. Fresh vegetables in the winter are a universal problem. A variety of apple that makes a glorious tart one day can be mealy and unacceptable the next. A good cook has to be endlessly alert and able to adapt, and one of the components of the art of cooking is surely the art of improvisation.

One way in which we are somewhat unusual is that our food and these recipes are extremely flexible in terms of menu planning. We don't give any sample menus here because we like the concept of mixing courses to suit your own tastes. At Al Forno, our grilled pizzas are offered as appetizers, but they're so big that people often share them or have them as a main course. It's not unusual for someone to order a salad, or an especially filling appetizer, as a main course.

We're famous, in fact, for our enormous portions, but we do try to make adjustments for the way people eat today. For example, we frequently suggest that two people split an appetizer, side dish, or main course that might be too filling for one. On our menu, we also distinguish between "small appetites," and "Al Forno appetites," and we always include at least one hearty all-vegetable entrée for non-meat-eaters.

In your own cooking, a grilled pizza might be enough for a dinner in itself, along with a salad. Similarly, pasta can be served in small amounts and treated as a first course, or in larger amounts as a main course. Mixed roasted vegetables make a terrific main course if you prepare enough of them. The important thing is the balance of flavors: A spicy appetizer like Clams Al Forno should be followed by something that's slightly more delicate—such as our Polenta Lasagne.

Balance is integral to good cooking and good menu planning. We're very conscious of it at Al Forno, not just in obvious ways like balancing a spicy food with a milder one, but in small things. We leave the lumps and peels in our mashed potatoes, for example, as a subtle, earthy contrast to the luxurious creaminess of the dish. We often finish off our grilled-sausage pizzas with a few slivers of green onion to give a cool crunch to the hot bite. We like the various parts of a dish to taste a little different—the flavor of the hot paprika on a chicken paillard will be stronger on the third bite than on the fourth and will be replaced by a bit of something completely different, like lemon aspic, a few bites later. It's important that a customer not tire of a dish, that it doesn't yield up all its secrets in the first couple of minutes. We like our food to continue to please and surprise as it is consumed.

Another basic aspect of our cooking is simplicity. We don't believe in complicated, arcane, improbable combinations of flavors or in tricky presentations. You'll never find peaches or caviar on our grilled pizzas, and we won't serve food that looks like a piece of modern sculpture. Our food looks like food; the flavors we combine have an inherent logic based on what we've tasted and read about and remembered. We try to use as few elements as possible in a dish, to refine it down to its essence. You'll see that our lists of ingredients are often very brief, and your response might be, "Is that all?" But in our recipes we want to convey one very elementary and perhaps obvious idea that's often forgotten: that food is wonderful in itself, and that the mission of the cook is to bring out its inherent goodness— to remember that a chicken is a chicken, a potato is a potato, and that the more those things taste like themselves, the better a dish will be.

We want this book to demystify cooking in general, and specifically the kind of Italian-based cooking we do at Al Forno. For us, cooking is indeed an art, and a challenging one, but it's always fun. If we're hungry, we're seldom too tired to cook, to fuss a little bit, to make something special for each other or for friends. We hope that even a portion of that joy and satisfaction will find its way into these pages and into the kitchens and hearts of everyone who uses the book.

CUCINA
SIMPATICA

STARTERS

Our menu at Al Forno is organized to give our customers great flexibility. We list together appetizers, soups, salads, and side dishes as suggestions for starters. If someone prefers to begin with pasta, that's fine too. We provide extra plates and serving spoons so that the dish can be shared.

Use the recipes in this book in the same way. Just as there are items in every category of our menu that one may order as an appetizer, there are recipes in every chapter of this book that would make good starters. Roasted Asparagus (page 142) can be a lovely beginning. Or, try your hand at the grilled pizzas. The important thing is to put together a menu with thought and care. There are no rules. If you want to serve the Clams Al Forno (page 26) as a main course, that's okay too. Increase the portions, serve with Al Forno's Mashed Potatoes (page 149), or pour the clams and their delicious broth over linguine. We encourage you to enjoy these recipes as you wish.

Antipasto Al Forno (page 27).

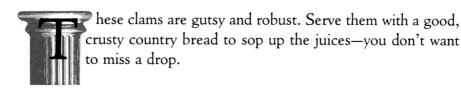
T hese clams are gutsy and robust. Serve them with a good, crusty country bread to sop up the juices—you don't want to miss a drop.

36 to 40 littleneck clams, cleaned and scrubbed
2 large onions (8 to 10 ounces), peeled, halved, and thinly sliced
1 jalapeño pepper, seeded and chopped
1/2 teaspoon dried red pepper flakes
3/4 cup dry white wine
1/2 cup water
2 tablespoons minced fresh garlic
1 1/2 cups chopped canned tomatoes in heavy puree
8 tablespoons (1 stick) unsalted butter, cut up
3 scallions, cut into julienne
1 lemon, cut into 6 wedges

1. Preheat the oven to 500 degrees.

2. Place the clams in a single layer in a baking dish.

3. Scatter all the remaining ingredients except the scallions and lemon wedges over the clams. Roast the clams for 9 minutes; turn them and roast for about 9 to 10 minutes longer, until they pop open. Discard any that don't open.

4. To serve, place 6 clams in each bowl and divide the broth among them. Serve piping hot, garnished with scallions and lemon wedges.

SERVES 6 AS AN APPETIZER

ANTIPASTO AL FORNO

The one constant in Antipasto Al Forno is paper-thin slices of prosciutto laid out in one layer on a platter. The antipasto can be expanded to accommodate the season and the number of people by varying the size of the platter and the amount of the ham, vegetables, olives, and cheese. The following suggestions create an impressive platter. Place the prepared and fresh foods in little mounds around the periphery of the prosciutto, taking care to alternate the colors and shapes.

For 6 hearty appetizer servings, you will need 12 paper-thin slices of prosciutto. Once sliced, prosciutto dries out very quickly. Buy it the day you plan to serve it, and keep it wrapped and refrigerated until you are ready to serve.

Lay the prosciutto out in a single layer on a serving platter, surrounding it with some or all of the following.

1/3 cup Grilled Caponata (page 146)
1/3 cup Grilled Peppers *Agrodolce* (page 152)
1/2 cup spinach, watercress, or arugula sautéed in olive oil
1 to 2 slices grilled onion from Grilled Onion Salad (page 52) or 6
   wedges Roasted Onions *Agrodolce* (page 155)
1/3 cup Tuscan Bean Puree (page 145)
1/4 cup Caramelized Garlic (page 167)
1 small piece fresh mozzarella (2 to 3 ounces), sliced and sprinkled
   with fresh cracked pepper
1/4 cup Spiced Olives (page 169)
6 wedges of Vinny's Frittata (page 30) at room temperature

SERVES 6 AS A HEARTY APPETIZER

SALMON POTATO CAKES
WITH TOMATO BUTTER

4 cups peeled and cubed red bliss or new potatoes
5 ounces smoked salmon, coarsely chopped (1/2 cup)
1 heaping tablespoon chopped fresh chives
1 egg, lightly beaten
Finely minced zest of 1 lemon
6 tablespoons sour cream
Pinch kosher salt
Pinch cayenne, or more to taste
1 cup canned tomato puree
8 tablespoons (1 stick) unsalted butter, softened

1. Cook the potatoes in boiling salted water until soft. Drain well and transfer to a mixing bowl. Mash the potatoes and set them aside to cool to room temperature.

2. Butter a baking sheet.

3. When the potatoes are cool, add the salmon, chives, egg, lemon zest, 3 tablespoons sour cream, salt, and cayenne. Mix well and form heaping tablespoons into oval cakes. As the cakes are formed, lay them out on the baking sheet. Refrigerate the potato cakes, covered, for 1/2 hour. The recipe may be completed up to this point several hours ahead of serving and refrigerated.

4. Preheat the oven to 500 degrees.

5. Bake the cakes until they are heated through, about 10 to 12 minutes. While the cakes are in the oven, heat the tomato puree in a skillet over medium heat. When the puree is hot, whisk in the butter over low heat to make a thin sauce.

6. Ladle a pool of the tomato butter onto 6 to 8 individual, heated plates. Top with 2 salmon potato cakes each, and garnish with the remaining sour cream.

SERVES 6 TO 8

DEEP-FRIED SAGE AND ANCHOVY SANDWICHES

We shared a plate of these tasty morsels with good friends at a country restaurant near Florence. Sage and anchovy, both strongly flavored ingredients, magically and harmoniously balance each other out.

Peanut oil for deep frying
36 large, fresh sage leaves
1 egg, lightly beaten
9 anchovy fillets, rinsed, patted dry, and cut in half
Flour for dredging

1. Heat the oil to 375 degrees in a pot appropriate for deep frying.

2. Dip 2 sage leaves in the beaten egg, sandwich an anchovy half between them, dip the "sandwich" again in the egg, and dredge lightly in the flour. Lay the sandwich on a piece of paper towel. Working quickly, repeat the process with the remaining sage leaves.

3. Drop the sandwiches into the hot oil, a few at a time, taking care not to crowd them. Cook for about 2 minutes, until golden brown. Remove with a slotted spoon, drain on paper towels, and serve hot.

SERVES 6 AS AN APPETIZER TIDBIT

VINNY'S FRITTATA

This is a lovely appetizer, a great addition to Antipasto Al Forno (page 27), or a nice light luncheon dish accompanied by a tossed green salad. You can serve it hot, warm, or at room temperature, the way it is enjoyed in Italy.

8 eggs
1/2 cup shredded fontina
1 cup freshly grated Pecorino Romano
3/4 cup heavy cream
2 cups cooked spaghetti or macaroni (5 ounces uncooked)
1 teaspoon kosher salt
1/4 teaspoon freshly cracked pepper
1 tablespoon chopped fresh parsley, tarragon, oregano, or sage
4 tablespoons olive oil

1. Preheat the oven to 350 degrees.

2. Whisk the eggs in a large mixing bowl. Add all the remaining ingredients except the olive oil, and stir to combine.

3. Heat the olive oil in a 9-inch cast-iron skillet. When the oil is very hot but not smoking, pour in the egg mixture.

4. Place the skillet in the oven and bake for 20 to 25 minutes, or until the frittata is set. Cool for 5 to 10 minutes before unmolding.

5. Run a rubber spatula around and underneath the frittata to loosen it. Slide the frittata onto a serving plate. You may serve it right away, or let it cool to room temperature.

SERVES 8 TO 10 AS AN APPETIZER,
6 AS A LIGHT LUNCHEON,
OR 12 OR MORE AS PART OF AN ANTIPASTO PLATTER

VARIATIONS: You can vary the frittata almost infinitely. For example, substitute cooked potatoes for the pasta, add cooked cauliflower or broccoli to the basic mixture, or experiment with different cheeses.

SOUPS

The most difficult part of this chapter was scaling down the recipes to feed a small group. When we think of soup, our nurturing instincts go into overdrive, and we always end up making a huge pot. No matter—it's just as good the next day and sometimes even better.

There's nothing more soul-satisfying than a bowl of steaming broth chock-full of vegetables and aromatic herbs. It is a wonderful way to begin a meal—or it can be the star attraction, accompanied by a salad and some great bread. Here are some of our favorites.

Pasta e Fagiole (page 42).

CHICKEN STOCK

Homemade stock is far superior to canned. Our stockpot is in continual service at the restaurant. At home, we keep small containers of rich stock in the freezer. It is the most important ingredient for a cook to have on hand.

12 large onions (3 pounds), root end removed, and cut up
5 to 6 carrots (1 pound), scraped and cut up
2 heads garlic, cloves separated, skin on
1 to 2 bulbs fennel, washed and cut up
3 to 4 stalks celery, washed and cut up
8 fresh tomatoes or 2 cups canned
8 pounds chicken necks and backs

1. Combine all the ingredients in a stockpot and cover with 2 gallons of cold water. Bring to a boil, skim off the scum that rises to the top, and simmer for 2 to 2½ hours, skimming as necessary.

2. Strain the stock through a fine mesh strainer, pressing down on the solids to extract as much flavor as possible. Discard the solids, and refrigerate the stock. When the stock is cold, remove the layer of fat that has hardened on the surface. Use the stock within 3 days or freeze for up to 2 months.

MAKES 2 QUARTS

Turnip Cream Soup with a Swirl of Apple Puree

We look forward to the first frost every year because it signals the arrival of Westport turnips at Walker's Roadside Stand. Coll Walker maintains that turnips, as well as Brussels sprouts and other fall vegetables, benefit from the frost: It makes their flesh sweeter. The Westport turnip thrives in Westport, Massachusetts, where the soil is sandy. Coll says they can be grown anywhere, but the sandy soil produces a smooth-skinned turnip. Coll's turnips, grown in Little Compton, Rhode Island, taste the same as those grown in Massachusetts, but they develop more tap roots.

What we call a Westport turnip is actually a Macomber rutabaga in the old seed catalogs. They are usually as large as yellow rutabagas, but their flesh is pure white. The seeds are no longer available, but Coll and a number of other local farmers keep their seeds from year to year.

George's inspiration in developing this recipe was largely visual. The white turnip puree is offset by the beautiful pink color of apple-sauce made with Empire apples. It makes a lovely presentation. Don't be put off by this recipe if Westport turnips and Empire apples are unavailable in your area. You may substitute yellow rutabagas and any nonmealy apple: McIntosh, Macoun, or Cortland. The colors may not be as dramatic, but your soup will be delicious.

4 tablespoons (1/2 stick) unsalted butter
2 large onions (8 to 10 ounces), peeled and thinly sliced
1 large Westport turnip (3 pounds), peeled and diced
2 teaspoons kosher salt
6 to 8 Empire apples (1 1/2 pounds)
2 cups heavy cream

1. Melt the butter in a stockpot and add the onion slices. Cook, covered, over low heat until the onions are very soft, about 15 to 20 minutes.

2. Add the diced turnip, 6 cups of water, and the salt. Raise the heat, bring the liquid to a boil, and reduce the heat to a simmer. Cook,

(continued)

covered, until the turnips are very soft and break up easily when pressed with the back of a spoon, about 1 hour.

3. While the turnips are cooking, quarter and core the apples, leaving the skins on. Cut each quarter in half horizontally. Combine the apples and 1½ cups of water in a small saucepan. Bring to a boil and cook, uncovered, until the apples disintegrate. Raise the heat and cook until the water has evaporated. As the liquid reduces, the sugars will concentrate. Keep a close watch on the apples, stirring constantly, as they can easily scorch. Puree the apples in a blender and set aside. You should have about 2 cups of puree.

4. Puree the turnips with their liquid in a blender and return the puree to a clean pot. Over low heat, add the cream. Bring to a boil, stirring constantly. Ladle the soup into heated bowls and garnish by swirling the apple puree in the center.

SERVES 8

SUMMER SQUASH SOUP
WITH GARDEN TOMATOES

I can remember how skeptical one of our staff members was when he saw us putting this soup together. He kept saying, "There's nothing in it." He was completely surprised to find that something so simple, made with so few ingredients, could taste so good.

This summer soup depends on fresh tomatoes and squash. When you have garden-fresh ingredients, you need little else to make a memorable dish. You can serve this chunky soup hot or cold. It is important to have your tomatoes at room temperature. We never refrigerate our native tomatoes; the cold seems to destroy their delicate flavor.

8 medium summer squash (2½ pounds)
1 large onion (4 ounces)
1 teaspoon kosher salt
3 fresh tomatoes (about 1 pound), at room temperature
1 cup heavy cream
6 fresh basil leaves

1. Trim the summer squash, discarding the ends. Cut the squash in half lengthwise, then cut the halves into 1/8-inch-thick half-moons.

2. Peel the onion and coarsely chop it.

3. Combine the squash, onion, and salt in a small stockpot with 5 cups of water. Bring to a boil and cook over medium-high heat until the squash becomes very soft and begins to disintegrate, about 30 to 35 minutes. A good deal of water will be absorbed by the squash, and some will evaporate, leaving behind a chunky puree.

4. Drop the tomatoes into a small pan of boiling water for 30 seconds. Remove from the water, core them, and slip off their skins. Cut the tomatoes in half horizontally, remove their seeds, and coarsely chop them. Set aside while you complete the soup.

5. Add the cream to the summer squash and bring to a boil. Taste to see if the soup needs additional salt.

6. Just before serving, shred the basil leaves.

7. Ladle the soup into heated bowls; garnish with chopped tomatoes and basil.

SERVES 6

VARIATION: To serve the soup cold, complete the recipe through step 3. Let the soup cool to room temperature, cover, and chill in the refrigerator for at least 2 hours or overnight. Complete step 4, add cold heavy cream to the summer squash, and serve the soup in chilled bowls garnished with the tomatoes and basil.

TUSCAN CABBAGE AND BEAN SOUP

This is a very hearty, rich soup. It will warm you right to the bone on a cold winter night. We serve it as an appetizer, but it would be a great main course accompanied by a tossed salad.

1 pound small navy beans, washed and picked over
1 prosciutto or ham bone
8 tablespoons olive oil
1/2 cup (3 ounces) pancetta, chopped (1/2 cup packed)
2 cups chopped fresh fennel
2 large onions (8 to 10 ounces), chopped
2 carrots, scraped and chopped
1 tablespoon chopped fresh garlic
1 teaspoon kosher salt
1 bay leaf
1 tablespoon ground cumin
1 teaspoon crushed red pepper flakes
1 small head savoy cabbage, shredded (about 10 cups)
1/4 cup johnnycake meal (see note)
1/2 cup freshly grated Parmigiano-Reggiano

1. Put the beans in a stockpot with the prosciutto or ham bone and 5 quarts of water. Bring to a boil, reduce the heat, and simmer until the beans are cooked through but still firm, 1 to 1½ hours.

2. While the beans are cooking, heat 4 tablespoons of olive oil in a large sauté pan. Add the pancetta, fennel, onion, carrot, garlic, and salt. Sauté, stirring frequently, until the vegetables soften and become aromatic, 15 to 20 minutes. Add the bay leaf, cumin, red pepper, and cabbage; continue to sauté for an additional 5 minutes.

3. Transfer the vegetables to the stockpot and cook for 30 minutes. You should have enough water in the pot to cover the vegetables. If not, add up to 4 cups more water.

4. Over very low heat, add the johnnycake meal a little at a time, stirring constantly. This will thicken the soup and enrich its flavor. After the meal is completely absorbed, simmer, stirring frequently, for 5 to 10 minutes.

5. Serve the soup piping hot, drizzled with the remaining olive oil and sprinkled with Parmigiano-Reggiano.

SERVES 8 TO 10

Note: If johnnycake meal is unavailable, substitute yellow cornmeal, adding it just after the vegetables in step 3. Simmer for 30 minutes and serve as described in step 5.

BLACK BEAN SOUP WITH
BUTTERNUT-SQUASH CROUTONS

Hot peppers vary greatly in intensity. We have used up to 8 jalapeños in this recipe. Test your jalapeños by tasting a very small piece, and vary the amount you use accordingly. Keep in mind that they will become tamer in cooking. Taste the soup just before serving; if the peppers have lost their zap, add some hot pepper sauce. We especially like the flavor of the West Indian hot sauces made with bonnet peppers.

4 tablespoons virgin olive oil
One 3-ounce piece prosciutto or 1/2 cup chopped pancetta
2 cups chopped onion
1 cup chopped carrot
1 cup chopped celery
2 tablespoons chopped garlic
4 to 8 jalapeño peppers, seeded and chopped
1 teaspoon kosher salt
1 pound black beans, washed and picked over
1 lemon
6 leaves fresh rosemary or 3 dried
2 to 3 teaspoons hot sauce (optional)
8 to 12 slices good-quality Italian bread
4 tablespoons (1/2 stick) unsalted butter, at room temperature
1 cup cooked and mashed butternut squash (see note)

1. Heat the olive oil in a heavy-bottomed stockpot and add the prosciutto or pancetta. Sauté over medium heat until the meat begins to brown, allowing some of its fat to melt into the oil.

2. Add the onion, carrot, celery, garlic, jalapeños, and salt. Sauté for about 10 minutes to soften the vegetables.

3. Add the beans and 12 cups of water, bring to a boil, lower the heat, and simmer until the beans are soft, 1 to 1½ hours. If you have used prosciutto, remove it to a cutting board, trim off as much fat as possible, chop the remaining meat, and return it to the soup. If the soup is too thick, add more water.

4. With a vegetable peeler, remove the thin yellow skin of the lemon, leaving behind the bitter white pith. Mince the lemon peel and add it to the soup with the rosemary. Taste the soup and add additional salt, if necessary. Add the hot sauce to taste.

5. Preheat the broiler, toast both sides of the bread, and spread with butter. Top the toasted bread with the squash and place under the broiler for a few minutes to heat through.

6. Ladle the soup into heated bowls, float a squash crouton in each bowl, and serve with a squeeze of fresh lemon. This soup is even better if served the day after it is made. If the soup has thickened, add a little water and reheat it slowly.

SERVES 8 TO 12

Note: We like to roast butternut squash rather than boil it. The flavor is more concentrated and nothing is lost to the pot.

Preheat the oven to 450 degrees. Cut the squash lengthwise, scoop out the seeds, and lay the halves, cut side down, on a baking sheet lined with foil. Roast uncovered for 40 to 50 minutes, or until the flesh is very soft. Scoop out the squash, discard their shells, and mash with a fork.

PASTA E FAGIOLE

1/2 pound navy beans, washed and picked over
3 tablespoons olive oil
1½ ounces lean pancetta, chopped (1/4 cup packed)
1 clove minced fresh garlic
1 stalk celery, chopped
1 cup chopped fennel
1 large onion (4 ounces), chopped
1 carrot, scraped and chopped
1/4 teaspoon crushed red pepper flakes
1 teaspoon kosher salt
1/2 cup chopped canned tomatoes
1 small sprig fresh rosemary, or 1/4 teaspoon dried
1 teaspoon minced fresh ginger
1 pound imported pappardelle (wide ribbon noodles)
3 to 4 tablespoons virgin olive oil
1/2 cup fresh grated Parmigiano-Reggiano (1½ ounces)
12 tender, inner leaves fresh escarole, cut into julienne strips or 12
    baby chicory leaves torn into bite-size pieces

1. Soak the beans overnight in water to cover.

2. Heat 3 tablespoons of olive oil in a large, heavy stockpot. Add the pancetta, and sauté until it begins to brown, 5 to 10 minutes. Add the garlic, and sauté 3 to 5 minutes.

3. Add the celery, fennel, onion, carrot, red pepper, and salt. Sauté for 10 minutes, on low heat, to soften.

4. Drain the beans, and add them to the stockpot with 8 cups of water, the tomatoes, and the rosemary. Bring to a boil, lower the heat, and simmer until the beans are soft but not mushy, 1 to 1½ hours.

5. Bring 5 quarts of salted water to a boil in a large pot.

6. Puree 3 cups of the soup with the ginger and return it to the stockpot. This will thicken the soup and give it a silky texture.

7. Drop the pappardelle in the boiling water and cook until al dente.

8. Ladle the soup into individual, heated bowls. Drain the pappardelle, and divide it among the soup bowls. Drizzle with the virgin olive oil, cover with a generous amount of grated cheese, and garnish with the julienned escarole or chicory leaves.

SERVES 8

Note: This soup is even better when reheated, so don't worry if you have some left over. Cover and refrigerate for up to 4 days. You can serve it with or without the pasta.

SALADS

We emphasize salads at both our restaurants. In fact, we are known to be fanatics about their handling, preparation, and presentation. First impressions are always important, and customers often choose salads to begin a meal. A good salad starts long before its arrival at the table. Be selective in choosing greens. This may not be a problem in summer when local produce abounds, but in fall and winter the choice is critical.

Once the goods are in the restaurant, proper handling is crucial. We often start a new employee at the salad station where we can quickly judge if he will work out just by the way he respects the ingredients. When a case of lettuce arrives, the first thing we do is trim away any bruised or damaged leaves. We carefully cut a thin slice off the root end of each head and stand it in about an inch of water in a pan. This allows water to be drawn up into the leaves, which keeps them crisp and fresh. After being misted with more cold water, the lettuce is draped with wet linen napkins and stored in the refrigerator until needed. This is the best way to store lettuce if you don't use it immediately. About an hour before serving, separate the leaves and soak them in very cold water to crisp them further. Drain and spin dry just before dressing. Any water left on the lettuce will dilute the dressing and make the salad soggy and bland. Be gentle in each step of this process so as not to bruise the greens. Following this procedure gives you a chance to scrutinize each leaf. There is no excuse for a salad made with blackened leaves or even the tiniest bit of rot or grit.

In this chapter you'll find salads for every season.

Spicy Clam Salad (page 47) with red and yellow Oven-Cured Tomatoes (page 178).

NATIVE TOMATO AND CORN SALAD

No matter how mild the winter, we always look forward to summer in New England. We're like little kids in a candy store when the first tomatoes appear at Coll Walker's country stand in Little Compton. Coll's farm is located on some of the most beautiful acreage in Rhode Island. It stretches from the roadside down a long, rolling hill to the mouth of the Sakonnet River. The view of the green fields ending at the river's edge with the Atlantic Ocean just beyond is breathtaking. We imagine that the salt air hovering above the fields in the morning fog adds to the taste of Coll's tomatoes. They are sweet and bursting with flavor.

This salad calls for freshly made croutons. We toast our croutons on a charcoal grill, giving them a slightly smoky aroma and taste. Make this salad in the summer when you are preparing a meal outdoors on the grill. The croutons are made like the Bruschetta on page 60; if a grill is not available, toast your bread under a broiler. Tomatoes weep and become watery if they are cut too long before serving, so make this salad just before you plan to eat it.

3 ears fresh sweet corn, hulled
1 small red onion
Four 1-inch-thick slices country bread
1 large garlic clove, peeled
8 medium summer tomatoes
7 tablespoons virgin olive oil
3 tablespoons balsamic vinegar
1/2 teaspoon kosher salt
8 basil leaves

1. Drop the corn in a pot full of boiling water. Cook for 4 minutes, refresh the corn under cold running water, and drain. With a sharp knife, cut the kernels from the cobs and place them in a bowl.

2. Peel the onion and cut it in half vertically. Cut out a V on the bottom of each onion half to remove the roots. Slice each half vertically into thin slivers and toss them with the corn.

3. Toast both sides of the bread on a charcoal grill or under the broiler and rub them with the garlic clove as if you were making Bruschetta. Drizzle the bread with 2 tablespoons of the oil, cut each piece into croutons about 1 inch square, and set aside.

4. Core the tomatoes, cut them into 6 vertical wedges, and cut each wedge in half horizontally. Add the tomato chunks to the bowl with the oil, vinegar, and salt. Toss to combine. Cut the basil into thin shreds and add to the salad with the croutons. Serve the salad immediately while the croutons are still warm.

SERVES 6

SPICY CLAM SALAD

36 littleneck clams, scrubbed
1 cup dry white wine
4 tablespoons (1/2 stick) unsalted butter
1 teaspoon minced fresh garlic
Pinch kosher salt
Six 5/8-inch-thick slices country bread
1 cup peeled, seeded, and chopped cucumbers
1/4 cup chopped red onion
1½ to 2 cups cooked corn from the cob (6 to 8 ears)
8 to 12 Oven-Cured Tomatoes (page 178), quartered, or 24 oven-
    cured cherry tomatoes
3/4 cup Hot Pepper–Infused Olive Oil (page 166)
1/2 to 1 cup red-wine vinegar
1/2 cup fresh Italian parsley leaves
1 tablespoon fresh thyme leaves
1/2 cup julienned scallion
6 cups mesclun or tender mixed lettuces, washed and dried

(continued)

1. Combine the clams, wine, and 1 cup of water in a stockpot. Cover, bring to a boil, and cook for 5 to 10 minutes, until the clams open. With tongs, transfer the opened clams to a large mixing bowl. Save the broth for another use (see note).

2. Melt the butter in a small saucepan with the garlic and salt. Brush both sides of the bread with the garlic butter. Toast under a broiler, turning once. Cut each slice of toasted bread into 6 to 8 croutons. Add to the mixing bowl with all the remaining ingredients. Toss to combine.

SERVES 6 AS A SALAD COURSE OR 4
AS A LIGHT MAIN COURSE

Note: We like to use the clam broth to make an *aglio-olio* sauce for spaghettini. Reduce the broth to 1 cup. Follow the recipe for Spaghettini with Watercress Aglio-Olio (page 113), substituting the broth for the chicken stock. Instead of the watercress, add 1/2 to 1 cup chopped fresh Italian parsley. Keep in mind that the clam broth will be salty, so you may not need any additional salt.

GRILLED SQUID SALAD

Rhode Island is dubbed the Ocean State. We have hundreds of miles of coastline and beautiful beaches, but unfortunately not a lot of great fish. We serve fish only on those rare occasions when we can get some that has been caught that day.

Squid is another story. We have been lucky to find a great source for local squid. We love to grill it for main courses and toss it with pasta, and we especially like squid salads.

2½ pounds squid, cleaned
3/4 cup virgin olive oil
2 stalks celery, chopped
3/4 cup chopped fresh fennel
1/2 cup freshly squeezed lemon juice
1/2 to 1 teaspoon minced fresh garlic
1/2 teaspoon Tabasco or other hot sauce, or more to taste
1/4 teaspoon kosher salt
1/4 cup chopped fresh Italian parsley

1. Prepare a charcoal fire, setting the grill rack about 4 inches above the coals.

2. Brush the squid bodies and tentacles with about 2 tablespoons of olive oil.

3. Grill the squid bodies about 3 minutes per side or until they puff up and lose their translucency. The tentacles may require an extra minute or two on the grill.

4. Remove the squid to a cutting board. Slice the bodies into rings and cut the tentacles in half.

5. Transfer the squid to a mixing bowl and toss with the remaining ingredients. Adjust the olive oil and lemon juice to taste.

SERVES 6

VARIATION: For a more substantial salad, slice 1 pound of new potatoes 1/8 inch thick, boil them until tender in 2 parts water and 1 part vinegar, drain, and toss into the salad. Cooking the potatoes in this manner prevents them from falling apart. It's an especially useful technique for salads.

SQUID SALAD WITH BALSAMIC VINEGAR, ORANGE, AND CILANTRO

2½ pounds squid, cleaned
2 large onions, peeled and cut into 5/8-inch-thick slices
3/4 cup virgin olive oil
2 stalks celery, chopped
1/4 cup balsamic vinegar
1/4 to 1/2 cup freshly squeezed orange juice
1/4 cup chopped fresh cilantro
1 teaspoon kosher salt
1 to 2 tablespoons bonnet-pepper hot sauce (see note)

1. Prepare a charcoal fire, setting the grill rack about 4 inches above the coals.

2. Brush the squid and the onion slices with some of the olive oil.

3. Grill the squid bodies about 3 minutes per side, or until they puff up and lose their translucency. The tentacles may require an additional 1 to 2 minutes on the grill.

4. Grill the onions until they are lightly charred, but cooked through, about 6 minutes per side.

5. Transfer the squid and onion slices to a cutting board. When cool enough to handle, cut the squid bodies into rings and the tentacles in half. Roughly chop the onions.

6. Combine the squid and onions in a large mixing bowl with the remaining ingredients. Toss to combine. Chill for at least 1 hour before serving.

SERVES 6 TO 8

Note: Bonnet-pepper hot sauce comes from the West Indies. It is very spicy but full of flavor. There are several brands available. You can find them in specialty grocery stores.

MUSHROOM SALAD WITH SHAVED PARMIGIANO

The next three recipes were inspired by an incredible dinner we ate at the Ristorante Diana in Bologna. It is a very old restaurant, always filled with stylish Italians. Seated beside us was a fashionable woman "of a certain age." She ordered a traditional vegetable soup, followed by an interesting-looking salad for her main course. She gave me the courage to vary the traditional order of an Italian meal and, yearning for something light after my pasta, I decided to try the same salad. It was one of the most extraordinary combinations I have ever experienced: paper-thin slices of ovoli mushrooms with shaved truffles and Parmigiano-Reggiano. It was dressed simply with a fruity green olive oil and a squeeze of lemon.

There is nothing quite like ovoli mushrooms. They are orange or red, with a delicate woodsy flavor. We decided to try adapting the salad with white cultivated mushrooms following the Ristorante Diana's method of presentation. The salad is not as exotic without the ovoli and truffles, but it is delicious. If you happen to have a fresh white truffle, by all means shave it over the mushrooms, but you needn't go to the expense to enjoy this lovely salad.

When you buy the Parmigiano-Reggiano, select a piece that is larger than the specified 4 to 6 ounces. You will be shaving the cheese over the mushrooms with a vegetable peeler, and it will be much easier to do this if you have a larger piece.

12 ounces fresh white mushrooms
1/4 teaspoon kosher salt
1/2 to 1 teaspoon fresh thyme leaves or 24 to 30 fresh Italian parsley
 leaves
One 4- to 6-ounce piece Parmigiano-Reggiano
2 lemons
6 to 8 tablespoons virgin olive oil
Fresh cracked pepper

1. Wipe the mushrooms to remove any dirt clinging to them, trim the stem ends, and cut the mushrooms vertically into paper-thin slices.

(continued)

2. Distribute half the mushrooms among 4 to 6 individual salad bowls, sprinkle with a pinch of salt each and the thyme or parsley, with a vegetable peeler, shave a layer of Parmigiano-Reggiano over the mushrooms. Repeat with the remaining mushrooms, salt, and Parmigiano.

3. Cut 1 lemon into 4 to 6 wedges for garnish. Squeeze the juice of the other lemon into a small bowl.

4. Drizzle 1 to 1½ tablespoons of olive oil over each salad, pour on the lemon juice, sprinkle with fresh cracked pepper, and serve garnished with lemon wedges.

SERVES 4 TO 6

GRILLED ONION SALAD
WITH SHAVED PARMIGIANO

This salad is great any time of the year, but it is a special treat in winter when good salad greens aren't readily available. Buy large yellow or red onions, about 3½ inches in diameter, weighing 12 to 14 ounces each. The large onions are much easier to work with and will give you a nicer presentation than the small ones that are sold prepackaged. You will need 1 onion per person.

In the summer, we do our grilling outdoors. In the winter, we set up a grill in our fireplace. It doesn't require any special equipment. We put a stack of bricks on each side of the fire basket, lay a grill over the bricks, and we're in business!

4 yellow or red onions (about 12 ounces each)
7 tablespoons virgin olive oil
1/2 teaspoon kosher salt
One 3- to 4-ounce piece Parmigiano-Reggiano
1/2 cup fresh Italian parsley leaves
Juice of 1 lemon

1. Prepare a medium-hot charcoal fire, setting the grill rack about 4 inches above the coals.

2. Trim the ends off the onions and cut them horizontally into 5/8-inch slices. Do *not* peel the onions. Brush the onion slices with 2 to 3 tablespoons of olive oil and sprinkle them with up to 1/2 teaspoon of kosher salt.

3. Grill the onion slices for 6 to 8 minutes per side or until the outsides are charred and the insides are completely cooked through. Transfer the slices to a platter and allow them to cool enough to handle.

4. Remove the skins from the onion slices and separate the slices into rings. Put a layer of overlapping rings into 4 individual salad bowls, garnish with some of the parsley leaves, and with a vegetable peeler, shave a layer of Parmigiano over the onions. Repeat the layers until all the onion slices are used.

5. Dress with the remaining olive oil and the lemon juice.

SERVES 4

BITTER GREENS WITH
HAZELNUT-GORGONZOLA VINAIGRETTE

5 ounces toasted and peeled hazelnuts (about 3/4 cup)
1/2 cup red-wine vinegar
1/4 cup balsamic vinegar
1 egg
1 tablespoon crumbled Gorgonzola
1 cup peanut oil
1/4 cup olive oil
2 medium heads radicchio (12 ounces)
9 to 12 medium heads endive (1¼ to 1½ pounds)

1. In a blender, puree the hazelnuts with the vinegars.

2. Add the egg and Gorgonzola. Puree for 1 minute.

3. With the motor running, add the oils in a slow, steady stream. This makes a very thick vinaigrette. You may have to whisk in the last bit of oil by hand.

4. Separate the leaves of the radicchio and endive. Toss the salad greens in a bowl with just enough vinaigrette to coat the leaves. If you have any leftover vinaigrette, cover it and refrigerate; it will keep for a few days.

SERVES 6 TO 8

CRUNCHY FENNEL SALAD
WITH SHAVED PARMIGIANO

This salad has a great contrast of textures. The crunch of the fennel is very satisfying with the creaminess of the Parmigiano-Reggiano.

2 lemons
4 large fennel bulbs
1/2 teaspoon kosher salt
One 4- to 6-ounce piece Parmigiano-Reggiano
1/2 cup fresh Italian parsley leaves
6 to 8 tablespoons virgin olive oil

1. Cut 1 lemon into 4 to 6 wedges and squeeze the juice of the other lemon. Set aside.

2. Cut off the feathery leaves and fibrous stalks of the fennel. You can chop the leaves and use them as a fresh herb. The stalks are not tender enough to eat, but they will lend a delicate flavor and fragrance to a homemade chicken stock. Trim the root ends and discard. With a sharp knife, cut the fennel into paper-thin vertical slices.

3. Distribute half of the fennel among 4 to 6 individual salad bowls, sprinkle with a little salt, cover with a layer of Parmigiano shaved directly over the salad with a vegetable peeler, and garnish with half the parsley leaves. Repeat with the remaining fennel, salt, Parmigiano, and parsley.

4. Drizzle the salads with the olive oil and fresh lemon juice. Serve garnished with the lemon wedges.

SERVES 4 TO 6

WARM POTATO SALAD WITH PANCETTA

7 tablespoons virgin olive oil
1½ pounds red potatoes, scrubbed
3 ounces pancetta, chopped (1/2 cup packed)
6 cups mixed lettuces, leaves separated, washed, and spun dry (see note)
1½ to 2 tablespoons balsamic vinegar
2 to 3 pinches kosher salt

1. Preheat the oven to 475 degrees, and brush two baking sheets with 1 tablespoon olive oil each.

2. Slice the potatoes into thin rounds, about 1/16 to 1/8 inch thick, and lay them out in a single layer on the baking sheets. Brush the potato slices with 2 tablespoons of olive oil, and top with the pancetta.

3. Roast the potatoes and pancetta for 15 to 18 minutes, until the potatoes are browned and cooked through.

4. About 3 minutes before you remove the potatoes from the oven, toss the lettuces in a bowl with the remaining 3 tablespoons olive oil, vinegar, and salt to taste. Keep in mind that the pancetta is salty.

5. Mound the lettuces in the center of a large serving platter and surround with the roasted potatoes and pancetta. Pour any oil left on the baking sheets over the salad. Serve immediately, while the potatoes are still warm.

SERVES 6

Note: This is a rich salad. For balance, use a mixture of firm, bitter lettuces such as chicory, escarole, endive, watercress, and radicchio.

Salad Al Forno

1 tablespoon Dijon mustard
1/4 cup plus 2 tablespoons red-wine vinegar
1/2 cup virgin olive oil
3/4 teaspoon kosher salt
6 cups finely shredded cabbage
3 ounces slab bacon, cut into 1/2-inch cubes (heaping 1/2 cup)
3 cups mixed bitter greens (radicchio, endive, escarole)
3 cups mixed leafy lettuces

1. Make a vinaigrette by whisking together the mustard and 1/4 cup vinegar in a mixing bowl. Slowly whisk in the olive oil. Add up to 3/4 teaspoon salt, and then fold in the cabbage. Set aside for 1 hour, at room temperature, so the cabbage has a chance to marinate. Or, you may prepare the recipe up to this point and refrigerate overnight. Allow the cabbage to return to room temperature before proceeding with the recipe.

2. Preheat the broiler, and lay out the bacon on a pie plate or baking sheet.

3. Broil the bacon, turning it once, for about 5 minutes, or until it browns.

4. Remove the bacon from the broiler, and immediately add the remaining vinegar to the pan. Swirl together, and pour the vinegar and bacon into the cabbage. Toss to combine.

5. Line a large platter or individual salad plates with the bitter greens and lettuces. Top with the cabbage mixture and serve immediately.

SERVES 6 TO 8

BRUSCHETTA, CROSTINI, AND POLENTA

Bruschetta and crostini are similar in that both are made of bread. Bruschetta is bread grilled over a charcoal fire, rubbed with garlic, drizzled with olive oil, and sprinkled with salt. It exemplifies the appeal of Italian food: simple ingredients combined in a straightforward manner. Because it consists of only four ingredients—bread, garlic, olive oil, and salt—each must be of the best quality, and the dish will be better than the sum of its parts.

In the summer we make bruschetta on the outdoor grill when it is already fired up to prepare a simple dinner. We serve it as an appetizer while the main course is cooking or as an accompaniment to grilled chicken, lamb, veal, or beef. In cold weather we find ourselves gathered around the fireplace where we improvise a grill over the logs to toast bruschetta. The intoxicating aroma of the garlic and olive oil is welcome in any season.

Crostini are made with slices of bread spread with butter, which are either grilled or toasted under a broiler. They are then spread with a variety of garnishes. Our crostini are spread with garlic butter. In their simplest form, they can be used as croutons for soups, or cut into smaller cubes and used as salad croutons. Variations of crostini are endless. We encourage you to try ours and then experiment.

Polenta is a specialty of the Veneto, in the northeastern part of Italy. Most often it is made with yellow cornmeal, although the more delicate white cornmeal sometimes accompanies seafood.

Clockwise, from top: Bruschetta with a Duo of Olive Purees (page 61); Veronese Grilled Polenta with Soppressata and Prosciutto (page 70); Grilled Chicken Liver Crostini (page 65); and Black-Olive Puree (page 170).

BRUSCHETTA

1 loaf good-quality Italian bread
2 to 3 garlic cloves, peeled
8 tablespoons virgin olive oil, or more to taste
6 pinches kosher salt, or more to taste

1. Prepare a charcoal fire, setting the grill rack about 4 inches above the coals.

2. Slice the bread 5/8 inch thick on the diagonal, discarding or snacking on the heels. The thickness of the bread is important in this recipe. We suggest 5/8 to 1 inch thick so the bread will be toasted on the outside but moist and chewy on the inside. An average loaf should give you about 12 slices.

3. Toast both sides of each slice of bread over the fire, remove from the grill, and rub one side of each slice with the garlic cloves. The texture of the toasted bread acts like sandpaper on the garlic, wearing it down so that its pulp and juice fill the pores of the bread. The more garlic you rub into the bread, the stronger the flavor.

4. Place the bread on a serving platter, drizzle lavishly with olive oil to cover, and sprinkle with salt. Serve immediately.

SERVES 6 TO 8

The following four recipes are variations of bruschetta. You may follow our suggestions or be creative and come up with combinations of your own. Keep in mind that bruschetta, or garlic bread, is a peasant dish. The simpler the ingredients, the better the dish.

BRUSCHETTA WITH A DUO OF OLIVE PUREES

Olive paste or puree can be found in most Italian specialty stores. It is so easy to prepare, however, that you can easily make your own. Keep it on hand for this recipe and for Bruschetta with Fresh Mozzarella and Black-Olive Puree (page 64); or, for a quick pasta sauce, toss a few tablespoons of olive puree into spaghetti or linguine *aglio-olio*.

1 loaf good-quality Italian bread
2 to 4 garlic cloves, peeled
8 tablespoons virgin olive oil, or more to taste
4 tablespoons Black-Olive Puree (page 170)
4 tablespoons Green-Olive Puree (page 170)

Follow steps 1 through 3 in the recipe for Bruschetta on page 60.

4. Place the toasted bread on a serving platter, drizzle with olive oil to cover, spread the black-olive puree on half the bread slices, and the green-olive puree on those remaining. Serve immediately.

SERVES 6 TO 8

This is a treat in summer when fresh tomatoes and basil abound. Forego this recipe in winter when tomatoes are bland and tasteless.

1 loaf good-quality Italian bread
3 garlic cloves, peeled
12 tablespoons extra-virgin olive oil
12 pinches kosher salt
4 ripe medium tomatoes (about 1¼ pounds), cored and cut horizontally into 1/4-inch-thick slices
24 leaves fresh basil

Follow steps 1 through 3 of the recipe for Bruschetta on page 60.

4. Place the bread on a serving platter, drizzle with olive oil, sprinkle with salt, and garnish each piece with overlapping tomato slices. Cut the basil into fine shreds and scatter over the tomatoes. Serve immediately.

SERVES 6

BRUSCHETTA WITH ARUGULA

The garlic and arugula make a wonderful marriage in this recipe. If you have some Tuscan Bean Puree on hand, spread it on the bruschetta and it will be even better.

1 loaf good-quality Italian bread
2 to 3 garlic cloves, peeled
8 tablespoons virgin olive oil, or more to taste
6 pinches kosher salt, or more to taste
1 cup Tuscan Bean Puree (page 145) (optional)
16 to 20 leaves arugula, cleaned

Follow steps 1 through 3 of the recipe for Bruschetta on page 60.

4. After you have rubbed the toasted bread slices with garlic, drizzle them with a little olive oil and sprinkle with salt. Spread each slice with about 1 tablespoon of the Tuscan Bean Puree, if desired, and top with the arugula. Drizzle with additional olive oil if you like and serve immediately.

SERVES 6 TO 8

BRUSCHETTA WITH FRESH MOZZARELLA AND BLACK-OLIVE PUREE

At the restaurant, the charcoal grill is next to the oven, making it convenient to grill the bread and then heat it in the oven with the mozzarella. At home, it would be more practical to toast the bread and melt the cheese under the broiler. It is a compromise, but the bruschetta will be delicious nonetheless.

1 loaf good-quality Italian bread
3 to 4 garlic cloves, peeled
8 tablespoons virgin olive oil, or more to taste
1 pinch kosher salt for each slice of bread
12 ounces fresh mozzarella (3 large), packed in water, thinly sliced (see note)
8 tablespoons Black-Olive Puree (page 170)

Follow steps 1 through 3 in the recipe for Bruschetta on page 60.

4. Place the toasted bread on a baking sheet, drizzle with half the olive oil, and sprinkle with salt. Top with the mozzarella slices and place under the broiler for 2 to 4 minutes. The cheese should melt and become a bit runny. Transfer the bruschetta to a serving platter, spread with the olive puree, and drizzle with the remaining olive oil. Serve the bruschetta right away, while the cheese is still hot.

SERVES 6 TO 8

Note: There is a world of difference between fresh mozzarella packed in water and the plastic-wrapped supermarket variety. Fresh mozzarella is much more widely available now than a few years ago, and it is worth the effort to find it. It has a short shelf life, so buy it when you plan to use it.

GRILLED CHICKEN LIVER CROSTINI

This is our adaptation of a traditional Tuscan dish. We like to grill the chicken livers and onions to give a smoky flavor to the crostini. The addition of fresh ginger lends an underlying mysterious taste.

1 pound chicken livers, trimmed
2 large onions (8 to 10 ounces), peeled
2 to 3 tablespoons virgin olive oil
12 tablespoons (1½ sticks) unsalted butter, at room temperature
2 leaves fresh sage
1/4 teaspoon minced fresh rosemary
1/8 teaspoon minced fresh ginger
1/2 cup freshly grated Parmigiano-Reggiano
1/4 teaspoon kosher salt (optional)
1 teaspoon minced fresh garlic
1 loaf Italian bread, cut into 1/2-inch-thick rounds
1/4 cup chopped fresh Italian parsley

1. Prepare a charcoal fire, setting the grill rack about 4 inches above the coals.

2. Skewer the chicken livers and slice the onions horizontally 5/8 inch thick. Brush the livers and onion slices all over with the olive oil.

3. Grill the onion slices about 8 minutes per side, or until they are lightly charred but cooked through. Grill the livers 2 to 3 minutes per side so that they are medium-rare or still pink inside.

4. On a cutting board, coarsely chop the livers and onions. Combine them in a bowl with 4 tablespoons of the butter, the sage, rosemary, ginger, and Parmigiano. Mash with a fork until you have a chunky texture. Taste and add the salt if necessary.

5. Fold the garlic into the remaining 8 tablespoons of butter and spread it on both sides of the bread slices. Grill the bread, toasting

(continued)

both sides. Spread each slice with some of the liver paste, and serve immediately garnished with parsley and additional Parmigiano.

SERVES 8 TO 10 AS AN APPETIZER

VARIATION: If grilling is not convenient, sauté the onions, chopped, in the olive oil until soft. Add the chicken livers and cook until they are medium-rare. Off heat, add 4 tablespoons of the butter, the sage, rosemary, ginger, and Parmigiano, mashing with a fork as in step 4. Follow step 5, toasting the bread under the broiler. Spread with liver paste and pass briefly under the broiler until hot.

CROSTINI SANDWICH WITH MUSHROOMS AND MASCARPONE

These sandwiches make a lovely appetizer. Our customers also like them served open-faced and topped with grilled veal tenderloins for a rich, satisfying main course.

14 tablespoons (1¾ sticks) unsalted butter
2 teaspoons minced fresh garlic
Eight 1/2-inch-thick slices country bread
2 tablespoons minced fresh shallot
6 to 8 cups (1¼ pounds) trimmed and sliced shiitake mushrooms (see note)
1 teaspoon fresh thyme, tarragon, or sage
3 tablespoons brandy or cognac
3/4 cup heavy cream
1/2 cup Mascarpone
1 teaspoon kosher salt
1/4 to 1/2 teaspoon fresh cracked pepper

1. Melt 6 tablespoons of butter with 1 teaspoon garlic in a large skillet. Brush this mixture on both sides of the bread. Place the bread in one layer on a baking dish and set aside.

2. Melt the remaining 8 tablespoons of butter in the same skillet. Add the remaining garlic and the shallots, and gently sauté until the garlic is soft, about 5 minutes. Add the mushrooms and herbs, raise the heat, and sauté until the mushrooms are cooked through, about 10 minutes.

3. Add the brandy and allow it to evaporate. Add the cream and Mascarpone, bring to a boil, lower the heat, and simmer for 2 minutes to thicken and reduce the cream. Add up to 1 teaspoon salt and the cracked pepper, and reduce the heat to keep the mixture warm.

4. Toast both sides of the bread under the broiler. Place 1 slice on each of 4 heated serving plates, divide the mushroom mixture among them, and top with the remaining toast.

SERVES 4 AS AN APPETIZER OR 8 AS AN OPEN-FACED SANDWICH TO BE TOPPED BY GRILLED VEAL TENDERLOINS OR CHOPS

Note: You may substitute white cultivated mushrooms if shiitake mushrooms are unavailable. The dish will not have the earthy taste of shiitakes, but it will be delicious just the same.

POLENTA

We use our local white cornmeal, or johnnycake meal, for polenta. It is stone-ground by our good friend Tim McTague at Gray's Grist Mill in Adamsville, Rhode Island. For more than a decade he has dedicated himself to keeping this dying art alive. He grinds the white flint corn in small quantities on ancient granite stones. The quality of his cornmeal is unsurpassed.

4 tablespoons olive oil
3 teaspoons kosher salt
2 cups cornmeal
4 tablespoons (1/2 stick) unsalted butter at room temperature

1. Bring 8½ cups of water to a boil in a large, heavy pot.

2. Add the olive oil and salt. Slowly add the cornmeal in a steady stream, stirring constantly. After all the cornmeal has been added, cook, stirring, over low heat until the polenta pulls away from the sides of the pot as you stir, about 20 minutes. The polenta should be thick, smooth, and creamy.

3. Stir in the butter and serve the soft polenta immediately as an accompaniment to stews, braises, poultry, sausage, or seafood.

SERVES 6

POLENTA LASAGNE

4 tablespoons olive oil
3 teaspoons kosher salt
2 cups coarse cornmeal
3 cups chopped canned tomatoes in heavy puree
6 tablespoons crumbled Gorgonzola
12 tablespoons Béchamel (page 110)
1/2 cup freshly grated Pecorino Romano (1 1/2 ounces)
1/2 cup shredded fontina (1 1/2 ounces)

Follow steps 1 and 2 for Polenta on page 68.

3. Pour the polenta into a 9-inch square pan, smoothing the top with a rubber spatula. The polenta will stiffen as it cools. After 2 hours, you will be able to cut the polenta into 12 squares, or refrigerate it (for up to 24 hours) until ready to use.

4. Preheat the oven to 375 degrees.

5. Cut each square of polenta in half horizontally.

6. Pour 2 cups of chopped tomato into a 9 × 12-inch baking pan. Cover with 12 polenta halves. Top with the Gorgonzola, half of the béchamel, and the remaining polenta halves. Sprinkle with the Pecorino Romano and fontina cheeses, drizzle on the remaining béchamel, and pour on the remaining cup of tomatoes.

7. Bake for 45 to 50 minutes.

SERVES 6 AS A FIRST COURSE

VERONESE GRILLED POLENTA WITH SOPPRESSATA AND PROSCIUTTO

O n a cold, winter day we had a memorable lunch in the hills outside Verona, hosted by a representative of Bolla wines. For one of the antipasti, we were served a plate of grilled polenta surrounded by paper-thin slices of Veronese salami and slices of what looked like raw bacon fat. There must have been shocked expressions around the table, so our hostess explained that the white slices were indeed pork fat, but it was not raw, it was cured. When she put a slice on top of the hot polenta, it softened and became translucent. We followed suit, trusting the wine to somehow counteract the effect of such a delicious indulgence.

We have adapted the idea to more available ingredients. The soppressata is similar to the Veronese salami. The prosciutto is our substitute for the cured pork. We love to serve the polenta with both meats; however, you may choose to use only one for a superb antipasto.

4 tablespoons olive oil
3 teaspoons kosher salt
2 cups coarse cornmeal
12 paper-thin slices soppressata
6 paper-thin slices prosciutto

Follow steps 1 and 2 for Polenta on page 68.

3. Pour the polenta into a 9-inch square pan, smoothing the top with a rubber spatula. The polenta will stiffen as it cools. After 2 hours, you will be able to cut the polenta into 12 squares, or refrigerate it (for up to 24 hours) until ready to use.

4. Prepare a charcoal fire, setting the grill rack 4 inches above the coals.

5. Grill the polenta squares 4 minutes per side. Transfer to a heated platter. Place 2 pieces of soppressata on 6 squares of polenta, and top each of the remaining squares with 1 piece of prosciutto.

SERVES 6

Note: Prosciutto and soppressata dry out quickly after they are cut. Buy the meats the day you plan to use them, and keep them wrapped until serving time.

Mike Lepizzera is the chef of Mike's Kitchen, a wonderful Italian restaurant in Cranston, Rhode Island. George and I eat at Mike's every chance we get. In fact, we are there so often we have become part of Mike's extended family and he part of ours. After enjoying his incredible food, Mike joins us at the table. We exchange recipes, tricks of the trade, and memories of Italy.

Besides being a fantastic cook, he is one of the most generous people we know. This is Mike's polenta. He gave us the recipe for this book. We think it's the best in the world.

1/4 cup virgin olive oil
1/2 pound (2 sticks) unsalted butter
1½ to 2 tablespoons chopped garlic
2 cups Chicken Stock (page 34)
1½ quarts half-and-half (see note)
1½ to 2 teaspoons kosher salt
12 turns of a pepper grinder
1 teaspoon crushed red pepper flakes
2 cups cornmeal
Pinch sugar
1½ to 2 cups freshly grated Pecorino Romano

1. Heat the oil and butter in a large, heavy stockpot. Add the garlic and sauté over low heat until it is golden.

2. Add the stock, half-and-half, 2½ cups of water, salt, and black and red peppers, and stir to combine. Raise the heat and bring to a boil.

3. Very slowly, add the cornmeal, stirring constantly. Lower the heat to maintain a gentle boil. After all the cornmeal has been added, continue to stir until it is thick and creamy, about 20 minutes.

4. Off the heat stir in the sugar and Romano. Serve right away with Garden Tomato Sauce (page 79) or the sauce from the Grilled and Braised Short Ribs of Beef (page 134). This polenta is also a great accompaniment to grilled sausages.

SERVES 10 TO 12 GENEROUSLY AS A FIRST COURSE

Note: You may substitute half heavy cream and half milk for the half-and-half.

GRILLED PIZZA

Early in our relationship, George and I tantalized each other with memories of certain foods we had experienced in Italy. We agreed that pizza in Italy was marvelous and completely different from what we grew up on in the United States. The crusts were thin and delicious. The toppings were sparse but intensely flavorful. And the best pizzas in Italy came out of wood-burning ovens, rather than the large deck ovens used here. As soon as you walked in the door of the pizzeria, you could see the fire burning in the oven and smell the smoke mingling with the aroma of tomatoes and fruity olive oil. Each person was served a whole pizza, about 10 inches in diameter, and ate it with a fork and knife.

I would describe Claudio's pizzas from Fiesole, and George would tell me about the wonderful pizzas made in the Campo dei Fiori in Rome. Our mouths would water and we would bemoan the fact that such delights were unavailable here.

One afternoon, at our local fish supplier, George got into a conversation with one of the crew who had just returned from Italy. He told George about the "grilled pizza" he had eaten in Florence. When George repeated the story to me I said that was impossible—I was sure the gentleman was confusing a grill with a wood-burning oven. Sure enough, he had seen the fire blazing in an open beehive oven and had the terminology confused. At first, George was disappointed. He had been ready to catch the next plane to Florence. Instead, he became so infatuated with the idea of grilling pizza that he decided to try it. Much to our surprise, the dough didn't fall through the grates, and within a week, we had a completely original menu item. We had successfully translated the flavors and textures of the pizzas we had so loved in Italy. In fact, our pizzas were more flavorful because the dough actually came in contact with the fire and smoke.

The grilled pizzas became quite the rage at the restaurant. Of all the things we do at Al Forno, it's our pizza that gets the most atten-

---

Grilled Pizzas, clockwise from bottom left: with Fresh Summer Herbs and Tomato (page 80); with Prosciutto, Egg, and Parmigiano (page 83); with Bitter Greens, Garlic, Tomato, and Two Cheeses (page 86); and Roman Style with Potatoes and Rosemary (page 84).

tion. On a recent concert tour, Billy Joel came to Providence. He created quite a stir when he arrived at Al Forno for dinner. He was so smitten by our pizzas he dedicated his first song at the concert to us and requested grilled pizzas every night he was here.

This chapter includes variations of grilled pizza for every taste. After you master the technique, try your own combinations. You'll find that you don't need recipes with exact measurements. Don't go for "the works." These pizzas should have a balance of flavors, above all; you want to taste the crust and each individual ingredient. Loading them up will not make them better, and with this grilling technique, the pizzas will burn before they heat through. The taste of each ingredient is important, so choose top-quality products.

PIZZA DOUGH

Grilled pizza is a sublime dish. Some people would happily foresake all other food for it. And why not?

To grill pizza successfully, you will need patience to master the technique. It may take a few practice runs before you get a pizza you want to serve, but you should persevere. Do not be timid about the preparation of this pizza. From start to finish the bold act will reward you with a first-rate pizza.

There are several obstacles that you will overcome with experience. To begin with, be sure you start with a hot wood or charcoal fire. Gas grills, even fueled by wood chips, will not do. They simply do not get hot enough, and the success of the dish depends on the unique flavor of smoke absorbed by the dough.

Build your fire on one side of the grill. During the cooking process you will want a cool area in order to add the toppings without burning the bottom of the crust. If you have a hibachi, build the fire on one side. For kettle-type grills, place a brick in the center of the bowl and bank charcoal on one half. If you have a small grill and cannot accommodate a 12-inch round of dough, divide it and make 2 or 3 small pizzas.

Be careful not to stretch the dough so thinly that holes appear. Don't despair, however, if small holes do appear. Though you cannot repair them, you can work around them. To avoid flare-ups, do not drizzle any of the oil or the filling into these holes.

When you are lifting the dough off the cookie sheet, it will invariably stretch; do not try to compensate for this by moving your hands apart. Work as close to the grill as possible so that the dough is without support for a minimum amount of time. If after 8 minutes the cheese has not melted and the topping is not bubbling, either you have been too cautious in your approach to the coals or you have used too much cheese and topping. More time on the grill will only dry out and toughen the pizza. The ideal crust should be both chewy and crisp.

The following recipe will make enough dough for four 12-inch pizzas. Each pizza will serve 4 as an appetizer or 1 as a main course.

They are so irresistible, however, that you may want to have extra dough on hand in case your guests demand an encore. Any leftover dough can be wrapped and refrigerated overnight, but remember to bring it to room temperature before grilling. We don't suggest freezing the dough. It toughens and does not spread easily to achieve the thin crust characteristic of grilled pizza. Before you become expert with the technique, make sure you have extra dough on hand for mishaps. After you are experienced, you'll be able to judge just how much dough to make. This recipe may be halved or doubled.

You can also use this dough to make grilled bread. Follow steps 1 through 3 of Grilled Pizza Margarita on page 80. In step 4, flip the dough over, drizzle it with olive oil, and sprinkle it with kosher salt, and fresh herbs if you like. Allow the underside to brown without charring. Transfer to a cutting board, cut into wedges, and serve immediately. The bread should be crisp with a chewy interior, a cross between pita and tandoori bread.

1 envelope (2½ teaspoons) active dry yeast
1 cup warm water
Pinch sugar
2¼ teaspoons kosher salt
1/4 cup johnnycake meal or fine-ground white cornmeal
3 tablespoons whole-wheat flour
1 tablespoon virgin olive oil
2½ to 3½ cups unbleached white flour

1. Dissolve the yeast in the warm water with the sugar.

2. After 5 minutes stir in the salt, johnnycake meal, whole-wheat flour, and oil.

3. Gradually add the white flour, stirring with a wooden spoon until a stiff dough has formed.

4. Place the dough on a floured board, and knead it for several minutes, adding only enough additional flour to keep the dough from sticking.

5. When the dough is smooth and shiny, transfer it to a bowl that has been brushed with olive oil. To prevent a skin from forming, brush the top of the dough with additional olive oil, cover the bowl with plastic wrap, and let rise in a warm place, away from drafts, until double in bulk, 1½ to 2 hours.

6. Punch down the dough and knead once more. Let the dough rise again for about 40 minutes.

7. Punch down the dough. If it is sticky, knead in a bit more flour.

MAKES ABOUT 24 OUNCES OF DOUGH OR ENOUGH FOR FOUR 12-INCH PIZZAS

GARDEN TOMATO SAUCE

This sauce is great on pizza or pasta.

3 tablespoons virgin olive oil ·
1 teaspoon minced fresh garlic
12 to 15 Italian plum tomatoes, peeled, seeded, and chopped
1/2 teaspoon kosher salt

Heat the olive oil in a heavy sauté pan. Add the garlic, and sauté until golden. Add the tomatoes and cook over moderate heat, stirring frequently, for about 10 minutes, or until the sauce begins to thicken. Add the salt. Set aside until ready to use. The sauce may be cooled to room temperature, covered, and refrigerated for up to 4 days, or frozen for up to 2 weeks.

MAKES ABOUT 2 CUPS OF SAUCE

GRILLED PIZZA WITH FRESH SUMMER HERBS AND TOMATO

6 ounces Pizza Dough (page 77)
1/4 cup virgin olive oil
1/2 teaspoon minced fresh garlic
1/2 cup mixed chopped fresh herbs (oregano, thyme, chives, and basil)
1/2 cup loosely packed shredded fontina
2 tablespoons freshly grated Pecorino Romano
1 garden tomato, sliced into thin rounds

Follow the instructions for Grilled Pizza Margarita (below), adding the herbs, cheeses, and tomato in step 4.

SERVES 1 AS A MAIN COURSE OR 2 TO 4 AS AN APPETIZER

GRILLED PIZZA MARGARITA

Y ou will note that the ingredients given in the following recipes are for individual pizzas. You may want to have different toppings on hand for a variety of pizzas. Feel free to invent your own combinations, but keep in mind that this is one situation where less is more. Use a judicious hand, and suppress the natural tendency to cover the entire surface of dough.

6 ounces Pizza Dough (page 77)
1/4 cup virgin olive oil for brushing and drizzling
1/2 teaspoon minced fresh garlic
1/2 cup loosely packed shredded fontina
2 tablespoons freshly grated Pecorino Romano
6 tablespoons chopped canned tomatoes in heavy puree
8 basil leaves

1. Prepare a hot charcoal fire, setting the grill rack 3 to 4 inches above the coals.

2. On a large, oiled, inverted baking sheet, spread and flatten the pizza dough with your hands into a 10- to 12-inch free-form circle, 1/8 inch thick. Do not make a lip. You may end up with a rectangle rather than a circle; the shape is unimportant, but do take care to maintain an even thickness.

3. When the fire is hot (when you can hold your hand over the coals for 3 to 4 seconds at a distance of 5 inches), use your fingertips to lift the dough gently by the two corners closest to you, and drape it onto the grill. Catch the loose edge on the grill first and guide the remaining dough into place over the fire. Within a minute the dough will puff slightly, the underside will stiffen, and grill marks will appear.

4. Using tongs, immediately flip the crust over, onto the coolest part of the grill. Quickly brush the grilled surface with olive oil. Scatter the garlic and cheeses over the dough, and spoon dollops of tomato over the cheese. Do not cover the entire surface of the pizza with tomatoes. Finally, drizzle the pizza with 1 to 2 tablespoons of olive oil.

5. Slide the pizza back toward the hot coals, but not directly over them. Using tongs, rotate the pizza frequently so that different sections receive high heat; check the underside often to see that it is not burning. The pizza is done when the top is bubbly and the cheese melted, about 6 to 8 minutes. Serve at once, topped with the basil leaves and additional olive oil, if desired.

SERVES 1 AS A MAIN COURSE OR
2 TO 4 AS AN APPETIZER

GRILLED PIZZA WITH SPINACH, GORGONZOLA, AND RAISINS

6 ounces Pizza Dough (page 77)
1/4 cup virgin olive oil
1/2 teaspoon minced garlic
1/2 cup loosely packed shredded fontina
2 tablespoons crumbled Gorgonzola
4 to 5 tablespoons Garden Tomato Sauce (page 79) or chopped
    canned tomatoes in heavy puree
8 to 10 fresh, tender spinach leaves, washed and patted dry
1 tablespoon raisins

Follow the instructions for Grilled Pizza Margarita (page 80), adding the garlic, cheeses, tomato sauce, spinach, and raisins in step 4.

**SERVES 1 AS A MAIN COURSE
OR 2 TO 4 AS AN APPETIZER**

GRILLED PIZZA WITH TOMATO, OLIVES, JALAPEÑOS, AND MOZZARELLA

6 ounces Pizza Dough (page 77)
1/4 cup virgin olive oil
1/2 teaspoon minced fresh garlic
1/2 cup loosely packed shredded fontina
2 ounces fresh mozzarella, drained and sliced
4 tablespoons Garden Tomato Sauce (page 79) or chopped canned
    tomatoes in heavy puree
1 jalapeño pepper, seeded and chopped
8 Kalamata olives, pitted and quartered

Follow the instructions for Grilled Pizza Margarita (page 80), adding the garlic, cheeses, tomato sauce, jalapeño pepper, and Kalamata olives in step 4.

SERVES 1 AS A MAIN COURSE
OR 2 TO 4 AS AN APPETIZER

GRILLED PIZZA WITH PROSCIUTTO, EGG, AND PARMIGIANO

6 ounces Pizza Dough (page 77)
1/4 cup virgin olive oil
3 tablespoons freshly grated Parmigiano-Reggiano
1/2 cup loosely packed shredded fontina
3 to 4 tablespoons Garden Tomato Sauce (page 79) or chopped canned tomatoes in heavy puree
1 egg (optional)
3 paper-thin slices prosciutto
1 tablespoon chopped fresh Italian parsley

Follow the instructions for Grilled Pizza Margarita (page 80), adding the cheeses and tomato sauce in step 4. Crack the egg onto the pizza, surround it with the prosciutto, and sprinkle with the parsley. The egg will cook sunny-side up on the crust.

SERVES 1 AS A MAIN COURSE
OR 2 TO 4 AS AN APPETIZER

GRILLED PIZZA ROMAN STYLE WITH POTATOES AND ROSEMARY

1/2 cup Al Forno's Mashed Potatoes (page 149)
1/4 teaspoon minced fresh rosemary, or 1/8 teaspoon dried
6 ounces Pizza Dough (page 77)
1/4 cup virgin olive oil
1 teaspoon minced fresh garlic
1 teaspoon chopped fresh Italian parsley
1/2 cup loosely packed shredded fontina
3 tablespoons freshly grated Parmigiano-Reggiano

Follow the instructions for Grilled Pizza Margarita (page 80). Immediately after lighting the fire (step 1), combine the potatoes and rosemary, and set aside. The potatoes may be leftovers, but they should be warm or at room temperature before you put them on the pizza. Continue with steps 2 through 5.

**SERVES 1 AS A MAIN COURSE
OR 2 TO 4 AS AN APPETIZER**

GRILLED PIZZA WITH BEAN PUREE, OLIVE PUREE, AND TOMATO

6 ounces Pizza Dough (page 77)

1/4 cup virgin olive oil

1 teaspoon minced fresh garlic

1 tablespoon chopped fresh herbs (parsley, thyme, chives)

1/2 cup loosely packed shredded fontina

3 tablespoons freshly grated Pecorino Romano

6 tablespoons Garden Tomato Sauce (page 79) or chopped canned tomatoes in heavy puree

3 to 4 tablespoons Tuscan Bean Puree (page 145)

2 tablespoons Black- or Green-Olive Puree (page 170)

Follow the instructions for Grilled Pizza Margarita (page 80), adding the garlic, herbs, cheeses, tomatoes, bean puree, and olive puree in step 4.

SERVES 1 AS A MAIN COURSE
OR 2 TO 4 AS AN APPETIZER

GRILLED PIZZA WITH BITTER GREENS, GARLIC, TOMATO, AND TWO CHEESES

6 ounces Pizza Dough (page 77)
1/4 cup virgin olive oil
1 teaspoon minced fresh garlic
1/2 cup loosely packed shredded fontina
3 tablespoons freshly grated Parmigiano-Reggiano
5 to 6 tablespoons Garden Tomato Sauce (page 79) or chopped
    canned tomatoes in heavy puree
8 tender leaves arugula, watercress, shredded radicchio, or sautéed
  tender broccoli di rape

Follow the instructions for Grilled Pizza Margarita (page 80), adding the garlic, cheeses, tomato, and bitter greens in step 4.

SERVES 1 AS A MAIN COURSE
OR 2 TO 4 AS AN APPETIZER

GRILLED PIZZA WITH RED-PEPPER PUREE AND SPICY PEPPER OIL

6 ounces Pizza Dough (page 77)
1/8 cup virgin olive oil for brushing
1/2 teaspoon minced fresh garlic
1/2 cup loosely packed shredded fontina
2 tablespoons freshly grated Pecorino Romano
6 tablespoons Red-Pepper Puree (page 93)
2 to 3 tablespoons Hot Pepper–Infused Olive Oil (page 166)
2 tablespoons chopped fresh Italian parsley

Follow steps 1 through 3 of the instructions for Grilled Pizza Margarita (page 80).

4. Using tongs, immediately flip the crust over, onto the coolest part of the grill. Quickly brush the grilled surface with olive oil. Scatter the garlic and cheeses over the dough, spoon on dollops of pepper puree, drizzle with pepper oil, and sprinkle the parsley over the entire surface. Proceed with the grilling instructions in step 5.

SERVES 1 AS A MAIN COURSE OR 2 TO 4 AS AN APPETIZER

WINE HARVEST–STYLE GRILLED PIZZA
WITH PROSCIUTTO

If you are lucky enough to be in Italy during grape-harvest season, look for the traditional sweet *schiacciata* or pizza made with red-wine grapes, sugar, and fennel seed. It is available in pastry shops and country bakeries. Based on the original, we have developed this grilled pizza, which can be enjoyed in any season as an appetizer or main course. It is a savory blend of sweet and sour—the Italian *agrodolce*—offset by the saltiness and richness of prosciutto.

TOPPING

3 tablespoons virgin olive oil
3 large onions (about 12 ounces, total) peeled, and sliced into thin vertical slivers
1/3 cup red-wine vinegar
3/4 cup pitted prunes
3/4 cup raisins
1/2 cinnamon stick
1/4 teaspoon fennel seed

PIZZA

12 ounces Pizza Dough (page 77) divided into 2 balls
5 to 6 tablespoons virgin olive oil
8 slices prosciutto

1. Heat the olive oil in a large skillet. Add the onion and sauté over low heat, stirring occasionally, until very soft and golden brown, about 20 to 25 minutes.

2. Add the vinegar, raise the heat, and allow the vinegar to reduce by half.

3. Add the prunes, raisins, cinnamon, and fennel seed along with 2 cups of water. Bring to a boil, lower the heat, and cook for 15 to 30 minutes, stirring occasionally, until the prunes fall apart and the mixture reduces to the consistency of loose jam. Discard the cinnamon stick. You can use the jam right away for pizzas or cool to room temperature and refrigerate, covered, for up to a week. Bring the jam to room temperature before topping the pizzas, so it will heat through.

4. Follow steps 1 through 3 of Grilled Pizza Margarita on page 80. Flip the dough, brush evenly with 1 tablespoon olive oil, spread with half the prune-raisin jam, and top with 4 slices of prosciutto. Drizzle with olive oil and proceed with the grilling instructions in step 5. As the raisin mixture heats through, the prosciutto on top will become warm and transparent.

5. Repeat with the remaining ball of pizza dough.

EACH PIZZA SERVES 1 AS A MAIN COURSE
OR 2 TO 4 AS AN APPETIZER

PASTA

Shortly before we opened Al Forno in January 1980, we were hesitant and anxious. In our new small space, we planned to serve a type of pizza we had eaten and loved in the ghetto in Rome. They were large pan pizzas with thick crusts and the most unusual toppings we had ever encountered. There were artichoke pizzas, pizza "bianca" covered with thin rounds of zucchini and herbs, and our favorite—pizza topped with paper-thin slices of potato dressed with olive oil and fresh rosemary. The pizzas were displayed at room temperature in a glass case. They were cut into squares, any size you liked, and sold by weight. We often carried our choices to the Tiber and enjoyed our picnic lunch by the river. As glorious as these pizzas were, we became increasingly worried that our new restaurant would be perceived as just another pizza parlor.

In an attempt to avoid facing the inevitable opening, the new responsibilities, and our mounting anxiety, we started thumbing through old issues of *Gourmet* magazine. In an article about Italy we found a photograph that changed the course of our lives. We saw in chiaroscuro a casserole of what looked like baked pasta. The lighting was dim; the background smoky and mysterious. The only clear color in the photo was a flash of red that was probably tomato. The top of the casserole looked crusty and charred as if licked by the flames of a wood-fired oven. Our imaginations raced as we started conjuring up what the pasta tasted like. The image was so enticing that we could almost smell the aroma from the steam curling above it.

We decided on the spot to change the format of our menu. That pasta was the kind of food we wanted to serve in our restaurant. That photograph evoked for us the new restaurant's possibilities.

Cappellini in Rich Chicken Broth Dusted with Parmigiano
(page 103).

BAKED PASTA

We began experimenting with baked pastas. We adapted the flavors and textures that were familiar to us from our travels in Italy. Pasta with four cheeses was my all-time favorite from the year I lived in Florence. In 1971 it seemed that every trattoria served its special version of this dish. It was usually prepared by combining cooked penne with a bit of tomato, cream, and fontina, Gorgonzola, Parmigiano, and Pecorino Romano cheeses. The resulting sauce was rich and creamy.

Our first version combined all the same elements. We baked parboiled penne with fresh cream, tomato, and cheeses until the individual quills that poked out of the sauce became lightly charred. The pasta actually became impregnated with the flavor of the cheeses, and we achieved the look and spirit of the photo that had so intrigued and inspired us.

On our menu the dish was simply called Pasta Al Forno, and it began ten years of variations on a theme.

The following recipes leave plenty of room for creativity. Try our suggestions, but feel free to experiment with new combinations as well. The variations are endless. Keep in mind that the most successful dishes are usually the least complex. Strive for balance and harmony in the textures and flavors.

Use a sturdy pasta, preferably one with ridges or *rigate*. The pasta should remain firm. We suggest using individual, shallow baking dishes. Large or deep casseroles increase the baking time, and that makes the pasta mushy and much less delectable. With individual baking dishes, the pasta cooks quickly enough to remain firm, the sauce thickens, and the uppermost noodles become a bit crunchy as they char in the high heat. If you must compromise and use a large baking dish, be sure it's very shallow—no more than 1 inch deep—so that the baking is increased by only 1 to 2 minutes.

Pasta in the Pink with Red-Pepper Puree

4 red bell peppers, charred and peeled (page 150)
1/2 cup chopped canned tomatoes in heavy puree
2 cups heavy cream
1/2 cup freshly grated Pecorino Romano (1½ ounces)
1/2 cup coarsely shredded fontina (1½ ounces)
2 tablespoons ricotta
1½ teaspoons kosher salt
1 pound imported conchiglie rigate (pasta shells)
4 tablespoons (1/2 stick) unsalted butter

1. Preheat the oven to 500 degrees.

2. Bring 5 quarts of salted water to a boil in a stockpot.

3. Halve the peppers, remove the seeds, and puree them in a blender. You should have about 1 cup of puree.

4. In a large bowl, combine all the ingredients except the pasta shells and butter.

5. Parboil the pasta for 4 minutes. Drain and add to the ingredients in the bowl, tossing to combine.

6. Divide the pasta mixture among 6 to 8 individual, shallow, ceramic gratin dishes (1½- to 2-cup capacity). Dot with the butter and bake until bubbly and brown on top, about 7 to 10 minutes.

SERVES 6 TO 8 AS AN APPETIZER

VARIATION: For a nice variation, add 2 Italian hot or sweet sausages that have been parboiled for 8 minutes, their skins removed, and coarsely chopped.

PASTA SAPORE PICCANTE

2 hot Italian sausages (3 ounces each)
2 cups heavy cream
1/2 cup Chicken Stock (page 34)
1/2 cup freshly grated Pecorino Romano (1½ ounces)
1/2 cup coarsely shredded fontina (1½ ounces)
2 tablespoons ricotta
2 jalapeño peppers, seeded and chopped
6 fresh sage leaves, chopped (see note)
1 teaspoon kosher salt
1 red bell pepper, seeded and thinly sliced
1 yellow bell pepper, seeded and thinly sliced
4 tablespoons (1/2 stick) unsalted butter, melted
1 pound imported penne rigate or rotini

1. Preheat the oven to 500 degrees.

2. Parboil the sausages in enough water to cover for 8 minutes. This helps rid them of excess fat and ensures that they will be fully cooked in the sauce. Drain the sausages and allow them to cool enough to handle; slice into 1/8-inch-thick rounds.

3. Bring 5 quarts of salted water to a boil in a stockpot.

4. In a large bowl, mix the sausages with the cream, chicken stock, cheeses, jalapeños, sage, and salt. In a small bowl, toss the bell peppers with the melted butter to coat.

5. Parboil the pasta for 4 minutes. Drain well and fold into the other ingredients in the large bowl.

6. Divide the mixture among 6 to 8 individual, shallow, ceramic baking dishes (1½- to 2-cup capacity). Arrange the pepper slices on top in concentric circles and bake until bubbly and brown on top, 7 to 10 minutes.

SERVES 6 TO 8 AS AN APPETIZER

Note: Though the sage provides a special flavor to this dish, it is not essential to its success. If you cannot find fresh sage, do not substitute dried. Simply eliminate it from the recipe.

PENNE WITH TOMATO, CREAM, AND FIVE CHEESES

2 cups heavy cream
1 cup chopped canned tomatoes in heavy puree
1/2 cup freshly grated Pecorino Romano (1½ ounces)
1/2 cup coarsely shredded fontina (1½ ounces)
4 tablespoons crumbled Gorgonzola (1½ ounces)
2 tablespoons ricotta
2 small fresh mozzarella cheeses, sliced (1/4 pound)
3/4 teaspoon kosher salt
6 basil leaves, chopped
1 pound imported penne rigate
4 tablespoons (1/2 stick) unsalted butter

1. Preheat the oven to 500 degrees.

2. Bring 5 quarts of salted water to a boil in a stockpot.

3. In a mixing bowl, combine all the ingredients except the penne and butter. Stir well to combine.

4. Drop the penne into the boiling water and parboil for 4 minutes. Drain in a colander and add to the ingredients in the mixing bowl, tossing to combine.

5. Divide the pasta mixture among 6 to 8 individual, shallow, ceramic gratin dishes (1½- to 2-cup capacity). Dot with the butter and bake until bubbly and brown on top, 7 to 10 minutes.

SERVES 6 TO 8 AS AN APPETIZER

CONCHIGLIE AL FORNO
WITH MUSHROOMS AND RADICCHIO

6 ounces shiitake mushrooms, cleaned and trimmed
8 tablespoons (1 stick) unsalted butter
1 teaspoon kosher salt
2 cups (2 medium heads) finely shredded radicchio
2½ cups heavy cream
1/2 cup freshly grated Parmigiano-Reggiano (1½ ounces)
1/2 cup coarsely shredded fontina (1½ ounces)
1/2 cup crumbled Gorgonzola (3 ounces)
2 teaspoons ricotta
6 leaves fresh sage, chopped (see note)
1 pound imported conchiglie rigate (pasta shells)

1. Preheat the oven to 500 degrees.

2. Bring 5 quarts of salted water to a boil in a stockpot.

3. Remove the stems from the mushrooms and reserve for another use. Slice the mushroom caps about 1/4 inch thick.

4. Heat 6 tablespoons of butter in a large skillet; add the mushrooms and 1/4 teaspoon salt. Sauté over medium heat, stirring frequently, until they are cooked through, 3 to 5 minutes.

5. In a large mixing bowl, combine the mushrooms, radicchio, cream, cheeses, sage, and remaining salt.

6. Parboil the pasta shells for 4 minutes; drain and add to the ingredients in the mixing bowl. Toss to combine.

7. Divide the pasta mixture among 6 to 8 individual, shallow, ceramic gratin dishes (1½- to 2-cup capacity). Dot with the remaining 2 tablespoons of butter and bake until bubbly and brown on top, about 7 to 10 minutes.

SERVES 6 TO 8 AS AN APPETIZER

Note: In the absence of fresh sage, do not substitute dried. As a substitute, choose one of the following:

1 tablespoon coarsely chopped fresh tarragon
1 teaspoon fresh thyme leaves
8 leaves fresh rosemary
1/4 teaspoon fennel seed

You may garnish with fresh Italian parsley, but do not cook the parsley in the pasta.

PASTA WITH CAULIFLOWER
IN A SPICY PINK SAUCE

3 cups chopped canned tomatoes in heavy puree
1 ½ cups heavy cream
1/2 cup freshly grated Pecorino Romano (1 ½ ounces)
1/2 cup coarsely shredded fontina (1 ½ ounces)
2 tablespoons ricotta
1 to 2 jalapeño peppers, seeded and chopped
1 teaspoon crushed red pepper flakes
1 teaspoon kosher salt
1 medium head cauliflower, coarsely chopped
1 pound imported conchiglie rigate (pasta shells) or penne rigate
3 tablespoons unsalted butter

1. Preheat the oven to 500 degrees and bring 5 quarts of salted water to boil in a stockpot.

2. In a mixing bowl combine the tomatoes, cream, cheeses, peppers, and salt.

3. Drop the cauliflower and pasta into the boiling water for 4 minutes. Drain, add them to the mixing bowl, and toss to combine.

4. Transfer the mixture to 6 to 8 individual, shallow, ceramic baking dishes (1 ½- to 2-cup capacity). Top with a portion of butter and bake for 7 to 10 minutes, or until bubbly and brown on top.

SERVES 6 TO 8 AS AN APPETIZER

PASTA WITH ASPARAGUS
IN A LEMON CREAM SAUCE

2½ cups heavy cream
1 teaspoon minced lemon zest
1/2 cup freshly grated Pecorino Romano (1½ ounces)
1/2 cup coarsely shredded fontina (1½ ounces)
2 tablespoons ricotta
3/4 teaspoon kosher salt
12 ounces fresh asparagus, trimmed
2 tablespoons unsalted butter, melted
1 pound imported conchiglie rigate (pasta shells) or penne rigate

1. Preheat the oven to 500 degrees.

2. Bring 5 quarts of salted water to a boil in a stockpot.

3. In a large bowl, combine the heavy cream with the lemon zest, cheeses, and salt.

4. Slice the asparagus 1/8 inch thick on a severe diagonal. Place the asparagus in a small bowl with the melted butter, tossing to coat thoroughly.

5. Parboil the pasta by dropping it into the boiling water for 4 minutes. Drain in a colander, then add it to the cream mixture in the large bowl.

6. Divide the pasta mixture among 6 to 8 individual, shallow, ceramic gratin dishes (1½- to 2-cup capacity). Top with the asparagus pieces, placing them in a circle around the outside edges of the baking dishes. Bake until the pasta is bubbly and hot and the asparagus begins to brown, about 10 minutes.

SERVES 6 TO 8 AS AN APPETIZER

Pasta Baked with Grilled Eggplant, Tomato, and Herbed Ricotta Pockets

1 cup ricotta
2 tablespoons chopped fresh Italian parsley
1/4 teaspoon ground fennel
4 leaves fresh rosemary or 2 leaves dried, minced
1½ teaspoons kosher salt
1 medium eggplant (1 pound)
4 to 5 tablespoons virgin olive oil
3 cups chopped canned tomatoes in heavy puree
1½ cups heavy cream
1/2 cup freshly grated Pecorino Romano (1½ ounces)
1/2 cup coarsely shredded fontina (1½ ounces)
1/4 teaspoon crushed red pepper flakes
1 tablespoon chopped roasted garlic (page 143)
1 pound imported conchiglie rigate (pasta shells) or penne rigate
3 tablespoons unsalted butter

1. Start a charcoal fire, setting the grill rack about 4 inches above the coals. If grilling is inconvenient, preheat your broiler to cook the eggplant.

2. Bring 5 quarts of salted water to boil in a stockpot and preheat the oven to 500 degrees.

3. Combine the ricotta in a small bowl with the parsley, fennel, rosemary, and 1/4 teaspoon salt. Set aside.

4. Slice the eggplant into rounds about 5/8 inch thick. Brush both sides of the eggplant slices with the olive oil and sprinkle with 1/4 teaspoon salt.

5. Grill or broil the eggplant slices for 3 to 4 minutes per side, until they are browned and cooked through. Transfer them to a cutting board and chop coarsely.

6. In a mixing bowl combine the eggplant, tomato, cream, Pecorino Romano, fontina, red pepper, garlic, and up to 1 teaspoon salt.

7. Parboil the pasta for 4 minutes, drain, and toss in the bowl with the eggplant mixture.

8. Divide the mixture among 6 to 8 individual, shallow, ceramic baking dishes (1½- to 2-cup capacity). Put a dollop of the herbed ricotta in the center of each pasta dish, top with a portion of butter, and bake in the oven for 7 to 10 minutes, until bubbly and brown on top.

SERVES 6 TO 8 AS AN APPETIZER

Pasta with Rapini and Pancetta in a Spicy Tomato Cream Sauce

1 small bunch (3 ounces) rapini, washed and trimmed (see note)
1/2 teaspoon crushed red pepper flakes
3 cups chopped canned tomatoes in heavy puree
1 cup heavy cream
1/2 cup freshly grated Pecorino Romano (1½ ounces)
1/2 cup shredded fontina (1½ ounces)
2 tablespoons pitted and chopped Kalamata olives
1 teaspoon kosher salt
1 pound imported penne rigate
3 ounces pancetta, chopped (1/2 cup)

1. Preheat the oven to 500 degrees.

2. Bring 5 quarts of salted water to a boil in a stockpot.

3. Coarsely chop the rapini and combine it in a bowl with all the remaining ingredients except the penne and pancetta.

4. Parboil the pasta for 4 minutes, drain, and toss it in the bowl with the rapini. Stir well to combine.

5. Divide the pasta mixture among 6 to 8 individual, shallow, ceramic gratin dishes (1½- to 2-cup capacity). Top with the pancetta and bake until bubbly and brown on top, 7 to 10 minutes.

SERVES 6 TO 8 AS AN APPETIZER

Note: Rapini or broccoli di rape is a pungent green that adds a zesty lift to this pasta dish. It can be found in Italian markets or well-stocked supermarkets.

BOILED PASTA

The remaining pastas in this chapter are simply boiled and combined with their sauces, not baked. For the most part, these are quick and simple preparations, in fact, many of the sauces can be put together in the time it takes to cook the pasta.

When you are cooking spaghettini or any string pasta, remember to drain it before it reaches the al dente stage. Toss it with its sauce over low heat for a few minutes. It will continue to soften and become impregnated with the flavors as it absorbs the sauce. If the sauce becomes too thick, simply add a few tablespoons of the pasta cooking water. This is how pasta is cooked in Italy, and it's a secret we discovered after years of research and practice.

The same rule applies to rigatoni and the sturdier pastas, but you have a bit more leeway, since they are not as delicate as string pasta and don't overcook as rapidly.

CAPPELLINI IN RICH CHICKEN BROTH DUSTED WITH PARMIGIANO

This dish is as sublime as it is simple. Drain the pasta while it is still a bit crunchy. It continues to cook and soften in its own heat after it is drained.

2¼ cups Chicken Stock (page 34)
1/2 pound imported cappellini
3/4 cup freshly grated Parmigiano-Reggiano (2 to 2½ ounces)

(continued)

1. Bring 5 quarts of salted water to a boil in a large pot.

2. Bring the stock to a boil in a large skillet and lower the heat to a gentle simmer.

3. Drop the cappellini into the water, and boil for 1 to 2 minutes. Drain, add the pasta to the skillet, and toss with the stock.

4. Working quickly, transfer the cappellini and stock to individual heated bowls. Top with the cheese and serve immediately.

SERVES 4 AS A FIRST COURSE OR 2 AS A MAIN COURSE

PASTA WITH LENTIL AND PROSCIUTTO SAUCE

When we're trying to come up with a new dish for the restaurant, we often dig into our pasts. George's dad made lentil soup for the family every Friday night. For variety, he would boil spaghetti and toss it into the soup, which he served drizzled with olive oil. For George, the predictable Friday dinner became a treat.

The following two recipes were inspired by that little piece of history. These are hearty pasta sauces, perhaps better suited to a main course than to an appetizer.

Ask your butcher for an end piece of prosciutto. Usually these pieces are less expensive, and they are fine for this sauce.

4 tablespoons olive oil
1 stalk celery, diced
1 carrot, scraped and chopped
1 large onion (4 to 5 ounces), peeled and diced
1 tablespoon minced fresh garlic
1 jalapeño pepper, seeded and chopped
1/4 teaspoon crushed red pepper flakes
One 3-ounce piece prosciutto or pancetta, chopped (1/2 cup packed)
1 teaspoon kosher salt
8 ounces (1 heaping cup) lentils
1 red onion
1½ pounds imported spaghettini or linguine fini
8 tablespoons (1 stick) unsalted butter, cut up

1. Heat the olive oil in a small heavy stockpot and add the celery, carrot, diced onion, garlic, jalapeño, red pepper, prosciutto, and salt. Gently sauté, stirring occasionally, until the vegetables are soft and aromatic, 15 to 20 minutes.

2. Add the lentils and 5 cups of water, bring to a boil, and simmer until the lentils are soft but not mushy and falling apart, 18 to 22 minutes. The sauce may be completed to this point and chilled in the refrigerator until ready to use.

3. If you have refrigerated the sauce, heat it slowly over a low flame. Bring 5 quarts of salted water to a boil in another large pot, and chop the red onion for garnish.

4. When the lentil sauce is hot, drop the pasta in the water and boil until it is still quite firm, 4 to 5 minutes.

5. Drain the spaghettini in a colander, then add it to the sauce with the butter. Toss the pasta in the sauce for 1 to 2 minutes until al dente. Serve very hot, topped with the chopped red onion.

SERVES 6 AS A MAIN COURSE

SPAGHETTINI WITH ANCHOVIES, WALNUTS, AND GARLIC

1/2 cup walnut pieces or halves
Two 2-ounce cans anchovy fillets packed in olive oil
1/2 cup virgin olive oil
2 tablespoons minced fresh garlic
1 pound imported spaghettini

1. Bring 5 quarts of salted water to a boil in a stockpot.

2. In a food processor, grind the walnuts to a fine powder, being careful to stop before turning them into nut butter.

3. Drain the anchovies; rinse under cold running water to rid them of excess salt, pat dry with paper towels, and chop.

4. Heat the olive oil in a large skillet. Add the garlic and anchovies and gently sauté, stirring often, until the garlic turns a rich golden color. The anchovies will dissolve and become almost a paste.

5. Immediately add 1 cup of water to the skillet, being careful not to burn yourself, as the oil may spatter. Raise the heat and boil vigorously until the liquid has reduced by half. Keep the sauce warm over very low heat while the spaghettini cooks.

6. Drop the spaghettini into the boiling water and cook until it is still quite firm, about 4 to 5 minutes. Drain and add to the sauce in the skillet. Toss for about 2 minutes over low heat until the pasta is al dente. Sprinkle the walnuts over the pasta, tossing to distribute the nuts evenly. If the pasta becomes dry, add 1 to 2 tablespoons of the pasta water.

SERVES 6 TO 8 AS AN APPETIZER
OR 4 AS A MAIN COURSE

Spaghettini with Spicy Lentil Sauce

More and more customers ask us for meatless dishes. This variation on the previous recipe uses the same basic technique but the ingredients change.

4 tablespoons olive oil
8 tablespoons (1 stick) unsalted butter
1 cup chopped fresh fennel
2 carrots, scraped and chopped
2 large onions (8 to 10 ounces), peeled and chopped
1 tablespoon minced fresh garlic
1 teaspoon kosher salt
1/2 teaspoon crushed red pepper flakes
1 teaspoon Hungarian sweet paprika
1 teaspoon Hungarian hot paprika
8 ounces (1 heaping cup) lentils
1½ pounds imported spaghettini or linguine fini

1. Heat the olive oil and 2 tablespoons of butter in a saucepan.

2. Add the fennel, carrot, onion, garlic, salt, and red pepper. Sauté until the vegetables are soft, about 15 to 20 minutes.

3. Add the paprikas and sauté for an additional 2 minutes to coat the vegetables.

4. Add the lentils and 5 cups of water, bring to a boil, lower the heat, and simmer until the lentils are soft but not falling apart, 18 to 22 minutes.

5. Bring 5 quarts of salted water to a boil, drop the pasta in the water, and boil until it is still quite firm, 4 to 5 minutes.

6. Drain the pasta in a colander and add it to the lentil sauce with the remaining butter. Toss for 1 to 2 minutes until the pasta is al dente. Serve immediately.

SERVES 6 AS A MAIN COURSE

very time we go to Florence, we have our first lunch at
Coco Lezzone, a small family trattoria serving traditional
food. If truffles are in season, I order farfalle with butter and
white truffles. If I'm feeling really decadent, I follow the pasta
with Stracchino cheese showered with a king's ransom of shaved truffles and a drizzle of fruity green olive oil. It is one of the richest, most
satisfying dishes imaginable—simply irresistible. George invariably
begins his meal with their macaroni and meat sauce. The macaroni
is sauced so lightly that its intensity mystifies us. Unable to wait for
the next trip to Italy to enjoy his favorite dish, George has come up
with the following meat sauce for pasta. I think the cooks at Coco
Lezzone would tip their hats to him.

1 large onion, peeled
1 carrot, scraped
1/2 bulb fresh fennel
3 tablespoons virgin olive oil
12 tablespoons (1 1/2 sticks) unsalted butter
1 tablespoon ground fennel seed
1 teaspoon kosher salt
1 pound ground pork or beef, or a combination of both
1/2 cup dry white wine
1/2 cup chopped canned tomatoes in heavy puree
1 1/2 pounds imported pasta (see note)
Small wedge Parmigiano-Reggiano for grating

1. Finely mince the onion, carrot, and fresh fennel. You may do
this by hand or in a food processor.

2. Heat the olive oil and 4 tablespoons of butter in a heavy-
bottomed pot. Add the minced vegetables. Sauté over low heat, stirring occasionally, until they are very soft and have almost melted into
a puree. This can take about 30 minutes and requires patience. The
vegetables must be soft before proceeding with the recipe.

3. Add the ground fennel seed and salt. Sauté for 2 minutes and then add the meat. Raise the heat and sauté, stirring, until the meat is no longer pink.

4. Add the wine and cook gently, stirring occasionally, until almost all the wine has evaporated, about 30 minutes. Add the tomatoes and cook for an additional 15 minutes, until they are absorbed into the sauce.

5. Bring 5 quarts of salted water to a boil in a stockpot.

6. Drop the pasta into the hot water and cook until it is still quite firm, 4 to 5 minutes. Drain and add the pasta to the sauce, toss for 1 to 2 minutes, until al dente. Cut up the remaining 8 tablespoons of butter and add to the pasta. Continue to toss until the butter melts and combines with the sauce. Serve immediately. Pass the Parmigiano-Reggiano for your guests to grate over their pasta.

SERVES 8 TO 10 AS A FIRST COURSE OR 4 TO 6 AS A MAIN COURSE

Note: This sauce is wonderful with rigatoni or penne. It is equally delicious with a lighter pasta like pappardelle, fettuccine, or lasagnette noodles.

VARIATION: You may substitute 1 pound ground veal for the pork or beef. In step 4, after the wine has evaporated, add 1/2 cup milk. Allow the milk to evaporate; then add the tomato and proceed with the rest of the recipe. The milk adds a creamy, rich texture to the sauce that works particularly well with veal.

Buttery Onion Lasagne

BÉCHAMEL

1 1/2 cups milk
3 tablespoons unsalted butter
3 tablespoons all-purpose flour
1/4 teaspoon kosher salt

FILLING AND ASSEMBLY

7 tablespoons unsalted butter
4 large onions (2 pounds), halved vertically and thinly sliced
1 teaspoon kosher salt
6 fresh lasagne noodles (see note and page 112)
1/4 cup heavy cream
1 cup freshly grated Parmigiano-Reggiano (3 ounces)

1. To make the béchamel, scald the milk in a small saucepan. Melt the butter in a heavy saucepan over low heat. Add the flour, and stir with a wooden spoon until the mixture is smooth. Continue to stir until the mixture has bubbled for 2 minutes. Take care not to allow the flour to darken.

2. Very slowly, pour the hot milk into the flour-butter mixture. Stir over low heat until the béchamel has thickened to the consistency of thick cream. Stir in 1/4 teaspoon salt, remove from the heat, and set aside. The béchamel may be made several hours ahead, cooled, and refrigerated. It will thicken as it cools; if you make it in advance, reheat it very slowly until it reaches spreading consistency.

3. To make the filling, melt 6 tablespoons of butter in a large skillet. Add the onions and salt, and sauté over low heat until the onions are very soft, about 25 minutes.

4. Preheat the oven to 400 degrees, and bring 5 quarts of salted water to a boil in a large pot.

5. Drop the noodles into the hot water, a few at a time, and cook for 30 seconds. Drain and refresh under cold running water to stop the cooking process and to prevent the noodles from sticking together. Repeat until all the noodles are cooked.

6. To assemble the lasagne, spread a few tablespoons of béchamel on the bottom of a 9-inch square baking dish. Drizzle the heavy cream over the béchamel. Cover with 2 overlapping lasagne noodles, half the onion mixture, a few more tablespoons of béchamel, and half the cheese. Add 2 more lasagne noodles and cover as before. Add the last 2 lasagne noodles, coat with a thin layer of béchamel, and dot with 1 tablespoon butter.

7. Bake for 20 minutes, or until the top is golden brown and the filling is bubbling hot. Allow the lasagne to cool for 5 to 10 minutes before cutting.

SERVES 6 TO 8 AS AN APPETIZER
OR 4 AS A MAIN COURSE

Note: There are very good-quality imported packaged lasagne noodles on the market that can be substituted for fresh noodles. However, do not use the heavy, curly-edged lasagne noodles widely available. They are too thick and rubbery for this dish.

VARIATION: Instead of the sautéed onions in the filling, you may substitute 1½ cups sliced, cooked, fresh artichoke bottoms or 1 pound trimmed and sliced shiitake mushrooms that have been sautéed in 8 tablespoons of unsalted butter.

FOOD-PROCESSOR PASTA DOUGH FOR
LASAGNE OR LASAGNETTE

These are the basic proportions for fresh pasta dough. The quantity of eggs is somewhat variable. If it is a humid day, or if your flour has a high moisture content, you may not need to add all the eggs. If you find the dough sticky, knead in more flour. The dough should be pliable without becoming dry.

2 cups unbleached flour
3 large eggs, lightly beaten

1. Place the flour in the bowl of a food processor fitted with the steel blade.

2. Add the eggs through the feed tube while pulsing.

3. When the mixture resembles large peas, turn it out onto a floured board and knead into a stiff dough. Knead in as much flour as the dough will absorb without becoming dry. Cover the dough with a kitchen towel, and allow to rest for 1/2 hour.

4. Set up a pasta machine, setting the rollers to their widest opening.

5. Divide the dough in half. If the dough is sticky, dust it with flour. Flatten one dough half with the heel of your hand, and feed it through the pasta machine. Fold the dough in half lengthwise, and feed it through the machine again. Repeat four more times. Dust the dough with flour if it sticks to the rollers.

6. Roll the sheet of pasta through each successive setting until you have passed it through the thinnest opening of the machine. Repeat the process with the remaining dough half.

7. Cut each sheet of dough into 9-inch lengths. You may use the dough right away.

MAKES 1 POUND OR ENOUGH FOR
8 TO 10 LASAGNE NOODLES

VARIATION: For lasagnette noodles, cut the pasta into 6-inch lengths. Cook 2 to 3 noodles per person. This makes a light, delicate pasta, ideal for George's Meat Sauce (page 108).

SPAGHETTINI WITH WATERCRESS AGLIO-OLIO

1/2 cup virgin olive oil
2 tablespoons minced garlic
1 teaspoon kosher salt
1 cup Chicken Stock (page 34) or water
1 pound imported spaghettini
2 cups chopped watercress

1. Bring 5 quarts of salted water to a boil in a stockpot.

2. Heat the olive oil in a large sauté pan. Add the garlic and sauté, stirring occasionally, until it turns a rich, golden color.

3. Immediately add the salt and chicken stock. Bring the liquid to a boil and reduce it by half. Keep the sauce warm over very low heat while you cook the spaghettini.

4. Drop the spaghettini into the boiling water and cook until it is still quite firm, about 4 to 5 minutes. Drain in a colander. Transfer the pasta to the sauté pan, adding the watercress and tossing for about 2 minutes until the spaghettini is al dente. If too much of the sauce is absorbed, add 1 to 2 tablespoons of the pasta water. Serve immediately.

**SERVES 6 TO 8 AS AN APPETIZER
OR 4 AS A MAIN COURSE**

VARIATION: In step 2, add 1 tablespoon each hot and sweet Hungarian paprika with the garlic. If you like spicy food, increase the proportion of hot paprika. Continue with the rest of the recipe, omitting the watercress. Garnish with freshly grated Pecorino Romano.

Linguine with Cabbage and Butter Beans

This is a cross between a soup and a sauce that is chock-full of vegetables.

4 tablespoons olive oil
8 tablespoons (1 stick) unsalted butter
1 cup chopped fresh fennel
2 carrots, scraped and chopped
1 large onion, chopped
1 tablespoon chopped fresh garlic
1 medium savoy cabbage, shredded
1/2 teaspoon crushed red pepper flakes
1 teaspoon kosher salt
8 ounces dried butter beans (small lima beans)
1 pound imported linguine
Pecorino Romano for grating

1. Heat the oil and 2 tablespoons of butter in a heavy-bottomed pot. Add the fennel, carrot, onion, and garlic, and sauté gently until the vegetables are soft. This could take up to 30 minutes.

2. Add the cabbage, red pepper, and salt, and sauté for about 10 minutes, until soft. Add the butter beans and 8 cups of water. Bring to a boil, lower the heat, and simmer until the beans are soft, 1 to 1½ hours. Add additional salt to taste.

3. Bring 5 quarts of salted water to a boil in a large pot.

4. Cook the linguine until it is almost al dente, 4 to 6 minutes. Drain and add it to the sauce. Toss together over low heat until the pasta is al dente. Fold in the remaining butter, and serve with freshly grated Pecorino Romano.

SERVES 6 TO 8 AS A FIRST COURSE
OR 4 AS A MAIN COURSE

VARIATION: Add a prosciutto bone to cook with the beans.

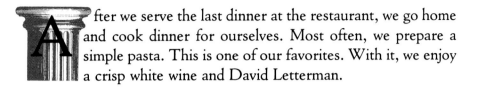

PASTA WITH PEPPERY PECORINO ROMANO

After we serve the last dinner at the restaurant, we go home and cook dinner for ourselves. Most often, we prepare a simple pasta. This is one of our favorites. With it, we enjoy a crisp white wine and David Letterman.

1/4 cup kosher salt
3/4 pound imported spaghettini or linguine fini
1 cup freshly grated Pecorino Romano (3 ounces)
15 to 20 turns of a peppermill (coarse grind)
2 tablespoons virgin olive oil

1. In a large pot, bring 5 quarts of water to a boil with the salt.

2. Cook the pasta until it is al dente, 4 to 6 minutes.

3. While the pasta is cooking, combine the cheese and the fresh cracked pepper in a small bowl.

4. Two minutes before you drain the pasta, combine the oil and 2/3 cup pasta water in a large skillet. Heat to a simmer over a low flame.

5. Drain the pasta and add it to the skillet. Add one-third of the cheese-pepper mixture. Toss to combine. Repeat with the remaining cheese mixture in two additions.

SERVES 4 AS A FIRST COURSE OR 2 AS A MAIN COURSE

VARIATION: In step 4, sauté 1/4 cup chopped pancetta in the oil. When it begins to brown, add the water, and proceed with the recipe.

RIGATONI WITH HERB-INFUSED
PIEMONTESE SAUCE

1/2 cup virgin olive oil
2 garlic cloves, peeled
2 cups canned tomatoes in heavy puree
1 cup loosely packed fresh basil leaves
2 cups loosely packed fresh Italian parsley leaves
1 teaspoon kosher salt
1 pound imported rigatoni
8 tablespoons (1 stick) unsalted butter, softened
Parmigiano-Reggiano for grating

1. Bring 5 quarts of salted water to a boil in a large pot.

2. Heat the olive oil in a skillet. Add the garlic cloves, and brown them without burning.

3. In batches, puree the tomatoes with the basil, parsley, garlic, and oil. Transfer to a bowl, preferably one made of stainless steel, that can rest on top of the pot of boiling pasta water.

4. Cook the rigatoni until they collapse, 10 to 12 minutes. For this recipe, they should be a little softer than al dente. While the pasta cooks, place the bowl over the boiling water. You want to warm the sauce without actually cooking it.

5. Drain the pasta, and add it to the sauce in the bowl with the butter. Grate some cheese over the pasta, and serve immediately. Pass additional cheese around the table.

**SERVES 6 TO 8 AS A FIRST COURSE
OR 4 AS A MAIN COURSE**

PAPPARDELLE WITH
PIEMONTESE SUGO DI POMODORO

We love the food and the people of Piemonte. This sauce was inspired by an incredible meal we had at Da Cesare in Albaretto della Torre, just south of Alba. Cesare and Silvana Giaccone own and operate this wonderful restaurant in a tiny hill town with a population of about sixty. There are no signs on the restaurant, but somehow people find it and this talented husband-and-wife team. Diners come from miles and contintents away to enjoy their food.

1 ½ cups Chicken Stock (page 34)
3/4 cup chopped canned tomatoes in heavy puree
8 tablespoons (1 stick) unsalted butter
1 pound imported pappardelle
1/2 cup freshly grated Parmigiano-Reggiano (1 ½ ounces)

1. Bring 5 quarts of salted water to a boil in a large pot.

2. Combine the stock, tomatoes, and 4 tablespoons of butter in a large skillet. Bring to a boil, and reduce by about 1/4.

3. Cook the pappardelle until almost al dente, 3 to 5 minutes. Drain, and add to the skillet with the remaining butter. Toss for 1 minute until the pasta is al dente. Add just enough cheese to thicken the sauce, and transfer to individual heated bowls.

4. Garnish each portion of pappardelle with the remaining cheese.

**SERVES 6 TO 8 AS A FIRST COURSE
OR 4 AS A MAIN COURSE**

GRILLS, ROASTS, AND BRAISES

George's love of wood fires is infectious, and we love the subtleties of food cooked on a grill or in a wood-fired oven. In the many years we've been in the kitchen together, we have experimented endlessly. George's fascination has resulted in our having several fireplaces at home—one with a built-in smoker—so that the experiments continue after hours. We may grill something fast and easy, we may grill a piece of meat to use in a quick Bolognese sauce for pasta, or we may use the grill to sear a piece of meat before slowly braising it. One way or another, fire usually plays a role in our cooking.

We have tried to demystify cooking with fire and stress the wide range of tastes possible through simple grilling. The uneven application of heat to the food, the smoke licking some parts and not others, the different types of woods used to make the fire—all contribute to the variety of flavors in each piece of meat, or pizza, or vegetable.

You don't need elaborate equipment—this is a primitive cooking technique that has been around for centuries. For outdoor cooking, a hibachi or kettle grill will do. Find natural hardwood charcoal. It is widely available at hardware stores and gourmet food shops. Start the fire with kindling—a few twigs and some paper. Do not use lighter fluid or briquettes, which contain petroleum by-products that will impart a chemical taste to the food. And don't even think about using a gas grill. The whole point of using wood or hardwood charcoal is flavor, and what you taste using a gas grill is the rancid residue left on the lava rocks from previous cooking.

We are including a variety of main-course ideas in this chapter—some grilled, some roasted in a conventional oven, and a few combining the two methods. There are recipes from our meals at home as well as from our restaurant kitchen. We hope you'll be inspired to use our combined method with one of your favorite recipes. Try searing beef-stew pieces over the fire rather than browning them in the pot. Do the same when preparing a chicken or pork stew. The important thing is to have fun cooking and enjoy the results.

Foreground: Rosemary Chicken (page 127); background:
Bruschetta-Stuffed Chicken Al Forno (page 130).

GRILLED VEAL TENDERLOINS WITH
GARLIC CROUTONS AND FRESH CORN

12 veal tenderloins, 3 to 4 ounces each (see note)
4 tablespoons virgin olive oil
1/2 teaspoon kosher salt
3 tablespoons balsamic vinegar
4 tablespoons (1/2 stick) unsalted butter, at room temperature
Six 5/8-inch-thick slices country bread
1 garlic clove, peeled
3 cups cooked fresh corn, cut from the cob (6 to 7 ears)
4 fresh tomatoes at room temperature, cut into 1-inch cubes

1. Prepare a medium-hot charcoal fire, setting the grill rack about 4 inches above the coals and heat a serving platter in a warm oven.

2. Brush the veal with 2 tablespoons of olive oil and sprinkle with salt.

3. Stir the balsamic vinegar and butter together on a hot serving platter, allowing the butter to melt into the vinegar.

4. Grill the veal for 3 to 4 minutes per side until medium-rare, transfer to the platter, and leave it to rest in the balsamic butter for 4 to 5 minutes. This allows the muscle tissue to relax, keeping the veal juicy and tender.

5. Toast both sides of the bread over the fire. On a cutting board, rub the toasted bread with the garlic clove, cut the bread into bite-size croutons, and scatter the croutons around the veal. Top with the corn, tomatoes, and remaining olive oil.

SERVES 6

Note: Veal tenderloins can be purchased at a good butcher shop or a supermarket with a well-stocked meat department. It may be a special order, so do call ahead to make arrangements. If tenderloins are unavailable, you may substitute veal steaks cut from the rib eye. Increase the grilling time 1 to 2 minutes per side.

GRILLED VEAL TENDERLOINS WITH GRILLED ONION RELISH

4 large onions (1 pound)
1/2 cup virgin olive oil
1 teaspoon kosher salt
1/2 cup balsamic vinegar
12 veal tenderloins, 3 to 4 ounces each (see note on page 120)
Six 5/8-inch-thick slices country bread
1 garlic clove, peeled

1. Prepare a medium-hot charcoal fire, setting the grill rack about 4 inches above the coals.

2. Cut the ends off the onions, peel them, and cut them horizontally into 5/8-inch-thick slices.

3. Brush both sides of the onion slices with 2 to 3 tablespoons of olive oil and sprinkle them with 1/2 teaspoon salt.

4. Grill the onion slices 6 to 8 minutes per side, until they are lightly charred and cooked through. Transfer the onions to a cutting board and chop coarsely.

5. Toss the chopped onions in a mixing bowl with the balsamic vinegar. Set aside while you grill the veal.

6. Brush the veal with 2 to 3 tablespoons of olive oil and sprinkle with the remaining salt. Grill the veal 3 to 4 minutes per side, until medium-rare. Transfer to a warm platter to rest for 4 to 5 minutes.

7. Prepare the grilled croutons as in step 5 of the previous recipe and lay them out on a serving dish. Cover the croutons with the onions, drizzle with the remaining olive oil, and top with the veal tenderloins and the meat juices that have accumulated on the platter.

SERVES 6

GRILLED DELMONICO STEAK WITH
TWO HOMEMADE CATSUPS

This is an Al Forno signature dish. It is served with a small mountain of mashed potatoes, tomato catsup, and yellow-pepper catsup—pure heaven for steak-and-potato aficionados. The 2-inch steaks in this recipe weigh in at more than a pound—a very generous portion.

1 cup balsamic vinegar
1/4 cup plus 2 to 3 tablespoons virgin olive oil
1 teaspoon minced fresh garlic
Six 2-inch-thick Delmonico steaks (about 22 ounces each)
1 teaspoon kosher salt
Spicy Tomato Catsup (page 171)
Spicy Yellow-Pepper Catsup (page 172)

1. Combine the vinegar, 1/4 cup of olive oil, and garlic in a baking dish large enough to accommodate the steaks. Marinate the steaks at room temperature, turning them occasionally, for 1 hour.

2. Prepare a charcoal fire, setting the grill rack 3 to 4 inches above the coals.

3. Drain the steaks, brush them with 1 to 2 tablespoons of olive oil, and sprinkle with salt.

4. When the coals are red-hot, and you can only keep your hand 3 to 5 inches over the fire for a count of three, place the steaks on the grill. Cook them for 8 minutes, brush the tops with olive oil, turn, and grill for an additional 8 minutes for medium-rare. Transfer the steaks to a warm platter and let them rest for at least 8 minutes before serving. This resting period makes the meat more juicy and tender. Serve with the two catsups and a mound of Al Forno's Mashed Potatoes (page 149).

SERVES 6

ROASTED SAUSAGES AND GRAPES

1½ pounds Italian hot sausage
1½ pounds Italian sweet sausage
3 tablespoons unsalted butter
6 to 7 cups (2½ pounds) red or green seedless grapes, stems removed
4 tablespoons balsamic vinegar

1. Preheat the oven to 500 degrees.

2. Parboil the sausages in water to cover for 8 minutes, to rid them of excess fat.

3. Melt the butter in a large flameproof roasting pan, add the grapes, and toss to coat.

4. With tongs, transfer the parboiled sausages to the roasting pan and push them down into the grapes so the sausages will not brown too quickly.

5. Roast in the oven, turning the sausages once, until the grapes are soft and the sausages have browned, 20 to 25 minutes.

6. With a slotted spoon, transfer the sausages and grapes to a heated serving platter.

7. Place the roasting pan on top of the stove over a medium-high flame and add the balsamic vinegar. Scrape up any browned bits on the bottom of the roasting pan, and allow the vinegar and juices to reduce until they are thick and syrupy.

8. Pour the sauce over the sausages and grapes and serve immediately, accompanied with Al Forno's Mashed Potatoes (page 149).

SERVES 6 TO 8

GRILLED AND BRAISED OSSO BUCO

On our rare days off, the fireplace in our kitchen is almost always ablaze. One evening, we decided to sear our country spare ribs over the fire rather than preparing them by the conventional method of browning them in a pot. We combined the grilled ribs with onions, sauerkraut, apples, and broth and braised them slowly until they were fork-tender. It was a great dinner; the flavor imparted by the fire was subtle but complex. We started experimenting with a variety of meats and found the results very satisfying. This method of cooking allows you to use less fat without losing a bit of flavor. And for an extra bonus, you won't get burned by oil spattering from the pot as the meat browns.

This cooking technique may seem like a lot of trouble, but it's worth it. The results are delicious.

Six 1½-inch-thick veal shanks
2 tablespoons virgin olive oil
6 tablespoons (3/4 stick) unsalted butter
2 ounces pancetta, diced (1/3 cup)
1 large onion, chopped
1 carrot, scraped and chopped
1 stalk celery, chopped
1 cup diced butternut squash (optional)
1 3-inch strip orange peel
1 3-inch strip lemon peel
2 cups chopped canned tomatoes in heavy puree
1½ cups Chicken Stock (page 34)
1/2 cup dry white wine

1. Prepare a medium-hot charcoal fire, setting the grill rack about 4 inches above the coals.

2. Brush both sides of the veal shanks with olive oil, and sear them

by grilling each side for about 4 minutes. Remove the veal from the grill and set aside on a warm platter.

3. Melt the butter in a flameproof casserole large enough to accommodate the veal shanks in one layer. Add the pancetta, onion, carrot, celery, and butternut squash. Sauté the mixture, stirring occasionally, until the onion is translucent, about 15 minutes.

4. Add the seared veal shanks and the remaining ingredients to the casserole.

5. Bring the liquid to a boil, cover the casserole, and reduce the heat to a gentle simmer. Braise the shanks for about 1½ hours, or until tender.

SERVES 6

Note: The traditional accompaniment to osso buco is saffron risotto. The most common garnish is gremolada, a mixture of finely chopped lemon zest, garlic, and Italian parsley. Our favorite nontraditional accompaniment is gremolada folded into Al Forno's Mashed Potatoes (page 149).

GRILLED AND BRAISED VEAL BREAST

This is an easy recipe for an economical, flavorful cut of veal. We like to serve it over buttered noodles.

1 tablespoon virgin olive oil
3 large onions, chopped
One 3- to 4-pound veal breast, bone in
One 12-ounce bottle beer
1/2 teaspoon kosher salt
2 garlic cloves

1. Prepare a charcoal fire, setting the grill rack about 10 inches above the coals (see note).

2. Preheat the oven to 400 degrees.

3. Heat the olive oil in a flameproof casserole or Dutch oven. Add the onion and sauté until it is translucent and cooked through. Set aside, off the heat.

4. Sear the veal on all sides over the fire, taking care not to allow the meat to char or burn.

5. Place the seared veal over the onion in the casserole. Add the beer, salt, and garlic. Bring the liquid to a boil, turn off heat, cover, and transfer the casserole to the middle rack of the oven.

6. Cook the veal until it is fork-tender, about 1¼ hours.

SERVES 4

Note: Searing the veal over the charcoal fire imparts a special flavor. It is worth the trouble, but if a grill is unavailable, brown the meat in the casserole. Heat 1 to 2 tablespoons of virgin olive oil, add the veal, and brown each side over high heat. Transfer the veal to a platter and discard the fat. Proceed with steps 2 through 6 of the recipe.

ROSEMARY CHICKEN

1 pound red, Maine, or California potatoes
4 tablespoons virgin olive oil
1/2 teaspoon kosher salt
3/4 cup chopped canned tomatoes
1/4 teaspoon fresh cracked pepper
5 tablespoons unsalted butter
4 double breasts of chicken (8 to 10 ounces each), skin on
4 large onions, peeled, halved vertically, and sliced lengthwise
1 teaspoon fresh rosemary or 1/4 teaspoon dried
1/4 cup chopped fresh Italian parsley
2 scallions, cut thinly on a diagonal

1. Preheat the oven to 500 degrees.

2. Cut each potato into 6 lengthwise wedges. In a large baking dish, toss the potatoes with 3 tablespoons of olive oil, 1/4 teaspoon of salt, 1/4 cup of tomatoes, and the pepper.

3. Roast the potatoes until tender, 25 to 30 minutes, stirring occasionally so the tomatoes do not burn.

4. About 5 to 10 minutes before the potatoes are cooked, melt 1 tablespoon butter and 1 tablespoon of olive oil in a 9-inch cast-iron skillet. Over high heat, brown the chicken breasts, 2 at a time, and remove them to a warm plate. In the same skillet, brown the onion over high heat in 2 batches, scraping up any bits of chicken.

5. Cover the cooked potatoes with the onion and chicken breasts. Sprinkle with the remaining salt. Top the chicken breasts with the remaining tomatoes, the rosemary, and the remaining butter.

6. Roast for 15 minutes, or until the chicken is fully cooked. Remove from the oven, and allow the chicken to rest for 5 minutes before serving. Garnish with parsley and scallion.

SERVES 4

GRILLED CHICKEN PAILLARDS WITH LEMON ASPIC AND SULTANAS

LEMON ASPIC

1½ cups freshly squeezed lemon juice, strained
2 envelopes gelatin
1/4 cup sugar

PAILLARDS AND ASSEMBLY

1/2 cup sultanas
6 to 8 skinned and boned double breasts of chicken (8 ounces each)
1/2 cup virgin olive oil
1/2 teaspoon Hungarian hot or sweet paprika
1 to 2 teaspoons kosher salt
12 cups mixed salad green (mesclun, radicchio, endive, salad bowl, green ice)
1/4 cup freshly squeezed lemon juice

1. Combine 1/4 cup of cold water and 1/4 cup of lemon juice in a small bowl. Sprinkle the gelatin over the surface of the liquid and let it soak for 5 minutes, until it has absorbed most of the liquid.

2. Bring the remaining lemon juice and sugar to a boil in a saucepan. Over very low heat, add the gelatin and stir until dissolved.

3. Pour the mixture into a 9 × 12-inch baking pan, chill in the refrigerator until it is firm, about 2 hours.

4. With a knife, slice the gelatin into 1/4-inch squares, and set aside.

5. Plump the sultanas in hot water to cover for 10 minutes. Drain and set aside.

6. Prepare a charcoal fire, setting the rack about 4 inches above the coals.

7. With a heavy, flat meat pounder (see note), pound the chicken breasts between sheets of plastic wrap or wax paper to an even 3/16-inch thickness. Brush the paillards with olive oil, sprinkle with paprika and salt, and set aside for at least 5 minutes.

8. Grill one side of the paillards until they stiffen and grill marks appear, about 1½ minutes. Turn, and grill for about 30 seconds. The second side may not appear to be cooked through, but the paillards will continue to cook after being removed from the grill. Transfer the paillards to a warm platter in one layer. (Stacking will steam and toughen them.) Set aside for 3 to 5 minutes.

9. Toss the greens together in a bowl with the remaining olive oil and lemon juice. Add a little kosher salt if desired.

10. Place the paillards on serving plates, surround with salad greens, pour over any juices that have collected from the paillards, and garnish with the lemon aspic and sultanas.

SERVES 6 TO 8

Note: There is an art to flattening chicken breasts or other meats for paillards. It is worth investing in a heavy, professional pounder. You will not get satisfactory results by substituting a bottle.

Strike the meat with the pounder, and draw it toward you in a continuous motion. Allow the weight of the pounder to do the work for you. You needn't strike with a great deal of force. Keep the bottom of the pounder parallel to the work surface so as not to create thin or thick spots. This takes a little practice, but with the proper tool, you will be successful.

VARIATION: We often substitute fresh cracked black pepper for the paprika—or use them in combination. Instead of the lemon aspic and sultanas, you can serve the paillards with one of our fruit chutneys—perhaps Spicy Cantaloupe Chutney (page 175) or Caramelized Cranberry-Apple Chutney (page 176).

For this recipe, we grill the bruschetta for the stuffing. This imparts a smoky flavor to the chicken, and it needs no other seasoning. If your outdoor grill is fired up for another portion of your meal, by all means grill the bread. If not, you can toast the bread over a wood fire in your fireplace. The most convenient method is to toast the bread under a broiler, in which case we suggest that you add 1 to 2 tablespoons of chopped fresh sage, thyme, or tarragon to the stuffing to enhance the flavor.

3 small chickens (2 to 2½ pounds each) or 6 Cornish hens (1 to 1¼
   pounds each)
Eight 5/8-inch-thick slices good-quality Italian bread
2 to 3 garlic cloves, peeled
1/2 to 3/4 cup virgin olive oil
1 teaspoon kosher salt
1 to 2 tablespoons chopped fresh herbs (optional)
1 cup Chicken Stock (page 34)
2 tablespoons unsalted butter

1. Preheat the oven to 450 degrees.

2. Rinse the chickens, inside and out, and dry them thoroughly with paper towels.

3. Toast both sides of the bread over a charcoal fire, in your fireplace over a wood fire, or under the broiler.

4. Rub both sides of the toasted bread with garlic. Cut the slices into 6 to 8 croutons each, and toss them in a bowl with 6 to 7 tablespoons olive oil and 1/2 teaspoon salt. Fold in the optional herbs.

5. Stuff the chickens with the crouton mixture. Bend the wing tips under the birds, brush the chickens with olive oil, and tie their legs together to keep the stuffing in place. Sprinkle the chickens with the remaining salt, put them in a roasting pan, and roast them for 45

minutes (30 minutes for Cornish hens). To ensure a moist bird, baste them 3 to 4 times.

6. Remove the chickens from the oven, and transfer them to a heated platter. Spoon off and discard the oil and chicken fat in the pan.

7. Deglaze the roasting pan by adding the chicken stock, bringing it to a boil, and scraping up any bits of chicken left in the pan. Allow the stock to reduce by half, then swirl in the butter. Pour the sauce over the chickens, and serve at once.

SERVES 6

MILK-BRAISED CHICKEN THIGHS
INFUSED WITH FRESH HERBS

This recipe was inspired by a traditional Tuscan dish of turkey braised in milk. Chicken thighs cooked in this manner are succulent and juicy.

12 chicken thighs (about 4 pounds)
3 tablespoons olive oil
1/2 cup Chicken Stock (page 34)
1 large onion, peeled and sliced
1 to 2 sprigs fresh rosemary
2 to 4 small branches fresh thyme
10 to 15 leaves fresh oregano
1 teaspoon kosher salt
1/2 teaspoon freshly cracked pepper
2½ cups milk
1 cup long-grain rice

1. Preheat the oven to 425 degrees.

2. Rinse the chicken and dry thoroughly with paper towels.

3. Heat the olive oil in a flameproof casserole. In batches, brown the chicken thighs, skin side only. Transfer them to a platter as they are browned.

4. Pour off the fat and add the chicken stock to the casserole. Over high heat, deglaze the casserole, scraping up any bits of chicken, and reduce the stock by half.

5. Return the chicken thighs to the casserole, sprinkling each with some onion, herbs, salt, and pepper.

6. Pour the milk over the chicken, and bring to a rolling boil. Transfer the casserole to the oven, and braise the chicken until done, about an hour. Check the casserole 2 to 3 times to be sure the liquid is maintaining a gentle boil (see note).

7. With tongs, transfer the chicken to an ovenproof platter, loosely cover with foil, and keep warm in the oven with the door ajar.

8. Measure the liquid in the casserole. You should have about 2 cups. If it measures more, reduce over high heat. If you have less than 2 cups, add water and return to the casserole.

9. Bring the liquid to a boil, add the rice, and simmer gently over low heat, uncovered and undisturbed, until the rice is tender, about 15 minutes. If the liquid evaporates too quickly, add 1/4 to 1/2 cup water. Surround the chicken with the rice, discard any herb branches, and serve piping hot.

SERVES 6

Note: The milk solids will clump and coagulate. Don't worry. They will be absorbed later by the rice.

GRILLED AND BRAISED SHORT RIBS OF BEEF

These short ribs make a delicious main course accompanied by bitter greens dressed with olive oil and red-wine or sherry vinegar. The salad offers a wonderful contrast to the richness of the beef.

The recipe also makes an abundant amount of pasta sauce. You can precede the ribs with a small portion of pasta dressed with the braising liquid and still have plenty of sauce for another meal. The leftover sauce may be frozen.

The ribs are seared over a charcoal fire to rid them of excess fat. You may accomplish the same thing by broiling the ribs on a rack in a roasting pan. Be careful not to char or burn the meat. Discard the fat that accumulates from broiling.

4 tablespoons olive oil
4 carrots, scraped and chopped
2 cups chopped fresh fennel
4 large onions, chopped
2 to 3 jalapeño peppers, seeded and chopped
6 to 8 large garlic cloves, peeled
1 teaspoon kosher salt
6 pounds short ribs
1 bottle dry red wine
6 cups canned tomatoes in heavy puree
3 cups Chicken Stock (page 34)

1. Prepare a hot charcoal or wood fire, setting the grill rack 10 inches above the coals; or preheat the broiler.

2. Heat the olive oil in a large Dutch oven. Add the carrot, fennel, onion, jalapeño peppers, garlic, and salt. Sauté, covered, over low heat until the vegetables are soft. This could take 20 to 30 minutes.

3. While the vegetables are sautéing, sear the ribs over the fire or under the broiler. Take care not to char or burn the beef as this may impart a bitter taste. Transfer the ribs to a platter.

4. Add the wine to the vegetables, and reduce over high heat until most of the liquid evaporates, 10 to 15 minutes.

5. In batches, puree the vegetables with the tomatoes. Return to the Dutch oven. Add the ribs and stock. Bring to a boil, cover, and simmer over low heat until the meat is fork tender, 2 to 2½ hours.

SERVES 6, WITH PLENTY OF SAUCE
LEFT OVER FOR ANOTHER USE

PORK SHOULDER BRAISED IN WINE
WITH TOMATOES AND PRUNES

Pork shoulder is a wonderful cut of meat. Don't be put off by the four-hour cooking time; slow braising will produce a succulent meal. This recipe is easy to prepare and requires minimal attention during the long simmering stage.

This dish is especially good served with Mike Lepizzera's Polenta (page 72). It is also delicious with Al Forno's Mashed Potatoes (page 149).

1 to 2 tablespoons olive oil
6 pounds pork shoulder
1 large head fennel, trimmed and cut up into wedges
4 large onions (1 pound), cut into 6 wedges each
6 carrots, scraped and cut up
2 garlic heads, peeled
1 tablespoon ground fennel seed
1 teaspoon kosher salt
10 turns of the peppermill
2 bottles dry red wine
2 cups Chicken Stock (page 34)
6 medium tomatoes (1¾ to 2 pounds), cored and peeled
11 ounces pitted prunes (about 1¾ cups)

1. Heat the oil in a large covered casserole or Dutch oven. Brown the pork on all sides. Add the fennel, onion, carrot, garlic, ground fennel seed, salt, and pepper. Toss the vegetables to coat in the oil.

2. Add the wine and stock, bring to a boil, lower the heat, and simmer, covered, until the meat is fork-tender and falling off the bone,

about 4 hours. Check often to be sure the broth is maintaining a very gentle simmer. A rolling boil will only toughen the meat and extract excess fat.

3. About 1 hour before serving, add the tomatoes. Thirty minutes before serving, add the prunes.

4. Skim off as much fat as possible.

5. Serve the pork surrounded by the vegetables and prunes with some of the broth.

Roasted Sausages and Grapes (page 123) and Al Forno's Mashed Potatoes (page 149).

One year, Bruce and Pat Tillinghast, chefs and owners of a lovely restaurant, New Rivers, in Providence, brought to our July 4th picnic some incredible sausages they had discovered at a producer in Roxbury, Massachusetts. The next day we contacted Victor Nosiglia and his son Dave at the Smokehouse. Their sausages are so good that we now develop recipes specially for them.

Because the Smokehouse's bonnet-pepper sausages are so spicy, we use them as an ingredient rather than eat them by themselves. They give this clam roast a serious kick while adding their unique flavor to the broth.

If you live in New England, by all means visit Victor and Dave's retail stores in Norwell and Wellesley, Massachusetts. Otherwise, find a good-quality Italian hot sausage and add fresh chopped bonnet peppers to the roast.

Choose small, tightly closed clams. Some clams open faster than others; that does not necessarily mean that they are of inferior quality—some clams just need a little coaxing. If most of the clams have opened, remove the stubborn ones to a cutting board. Hold each clam hinge-side down between your thumb and forefinger. Wedge the blade of a paring knife between the shells and apply a little pressure. If the clam does not readily open, you should discard it.

The clam roast is especially nice served with a mound of Al Forno's Mashed Potatoes (page 149).

4 bonnet-pepper sausages (or 1 pound hot Italian sausage)
4 large onions (1 pound)
48 littleneck clams, cleaned and scrubbed
1 jalapeño pepper, seeded and chopped
1 to 2 bonnet peppers, seeded and chopped (optional)
2 medium heads endive, coarsely chopped (1 ½ to 2 cups)
1/2 teaspoon dried red pepper flakes (optional)
3/4 cup dry white wine
2 tablespoons minced fresh garlic

1½ cups chopped canned tomatoes in heavy puree
8 tablespoons (1 stick) unsalted butter, cut up
3 scallions, cut into fine julienne
1 lemon, quartered

1. Preheat the oven to 500 degrees.

2. Drop the sausages in boiling water to cover and parboil for 8 minutes to rid them of excess fat. Drain and set aside on a cutting board. Allow the sausages to cool for about 10 minutes, then cut them on a diagonal into 1/2-inch-thick slices.

3. Peel the onions, cut them in half vertically, and cut a V in the bottom of each half to remove the root. Slice each half into thin vertical slivers.

4. Lay out the clams in a single layer in a flameproof baking dish or roasting pan. Top the clams with all the remaining ingredients except the scallion and lemon wedges.

5. Bring the liquid to a boil on top of the stove over high heat, then put the pan in the oven. Roast the clams for 8 minutes. Turn and roast for about 5 to 10 minutes longer, until they open.

6. Place 12 clams in each of 4 large heated bowls and pour the broth over them, evenly distributing the onions, tomatoes, and sausages. Garnish with julienned scallion and lemon wedges.

SERVES 4

Note: If you are preparing this dish for a dinner party, you can parboil the sausages ahead of time and chill them, uncut, in the refrigerator. In a bowl or plastic container, combine the onion slivers, chopped jalapeños, chopped bonnet peppers, chopped endive, red pepper flakes, wine, minced garlic, chopped tomatoes, and butter. Keep everything well chilled until you are ready to combine the ingredients and roast them. When you are ready to cook, slice the sausages and proceed with steps 4 through 6.

VEGETABLES

I n Italy, vegetables are held in high esteem. Every restaurant offers a selection, served at room temperature, as part of its antipasti. Even in most bars serving little *panini,* or sandwiches, there is usually a filling made with sautéed greens, grilled eggplant, or sautéed zucchini, or perhaps fresh tomatoes, basil, and mozzarella drizzled with fruity green olive oil. Being a vegetable lover myself, I often order a sampling from the antipasto table as my main course. And, for a quick lunch on the run, I can't resist the vegetable panini.

Vegetables are featured prominently at Al Forno. Our antipasto includes several tastes of different vegetable preparations. We offer seasonal roasted vegetables as a main course or appetizer. And we can hardly keep up with the demand for our mashed potatoes. Rather than using vegetables as a garnish, we accompany all of our main courses with a variety, cooked in the oven or on the grill. Often, customers order a particular main course for the selection of vegetables served with it. Then, there's the Veggie Entree—at least eight different vegetables, all cooked to order. It's a showstopper; even died-in-the-wool meat lovers are impressed! In the summer, when our local farmers are at full tilt, vegetables become the star attraction on our menu. Juicy ripe tomatoes are stuffed with Silver Queen corn and surrounded by mashed potatoes for a memorable meal.

Use the recipes in this chapter any way you like. Many of them can be combined to make a main course. Or, you may want to begin your meal with a small portion of fresh roasted asparagus or corn fritters. You may find yourself starting to rethink the role of vegetables in your menus. The roasted vegetables are a snap to cook, and they make a lovely meal. For antipasti, the possibilities are limitless.

Roasted Vegetables (pages 142–143).

ROASTED VEGETABLES

Our method of high-heat roasting caramelizes the natural sugars and intensifies the flavor of most vegetables. This method works well with all the vegetables we have tried; the only variable is whether to brush the vegetables with olive oil. Beans whose pods are discarded are roasted dry. Those vegetables that have no such natural protection are brushed lightly with olive oil.

ROASTED ASPARAGUS

1 1/2 pounds fresh asparagus, trimmed
2 to 3 tablespoons virgin olive oil
1/8 teaspoon kosher salt, or more to taste
2 tablespoons unsalted butter (optional)

1. Preheat the oven to 500 degrees.

2. Spread the asparagus out on a baking sheet in a single layer and brush them with the olive oil. Sprinkle with salt and roast the asparagus in the upper third of the oven until the spears are tender when pierced with the tip of a knife, about 10 to 12 minutes, depending on their thickness.

3. Remove the baking sheet from the oven. Immediately place the butter on a corner of the hot baking sheet to melt. With tongs, transfer the asparagus to a serving platter. Pour the melted butter over the asparagus and serve. (They are also delicious without the butter.)

SERVES 6

VARIATIONS: Other vegetables that benefit from this method:

1½ pounds haricots verts (roast for 5 minutes)
1½ pounds green or wax beans (roast for 10 to 12 minutes)
1½ pounds sugar snap peas (roast for 8 to 10 minutes)
2 to 3 sweet red, yellow, or orange peppers, halved and seeded (roast for 10 to 12 minutes and do not serve with butter)
1 bunch carrots, scraped and cut into 1/4-inch diagonal slices (roast for 10 to 12 minutes)
1 pound baby carrots, scraped (roast 8 to 10 minutes)
1 pound scallions, trimmed (roast for 10 to 12 minutes)
3 to 4 medium cucumbers, peeled, seeded, and sliced 1/4 inch thick (roast for 8 to 10 minutes)
6 to 8 hot finger peppers (roast 8 minutes)
1½ pounds zucchini or summer squash (roast 8 to 10 minutes)
1 pound Brussels sprouts, parboiled 2 minutes (roast 10 to 12 minutes)
1 pound white radishes (roast 8 minutes)
1½ pounds sweet potatoes or red bliss potatoes, sliced thin (roast 10 to 12 minutes)

Fan the following vegetables. Do not remove their husks, skins, pods, etc., until just before eating.

1½ pounds fresh fava beans (roast for 10 to 12 minutes)
1 pound shallots (roast for 10 to 12 minutes)
1½ pounds pearl onions (roast for 12 to 14 minutes)
4 to 6 ears fresh corn (roast for 8 to 10 minutes)
3 pounds sweet peas (roast for 8 to 10 minutes)
3 pounds small beets (roast for 40 minutes covered and 10 minutes uncovered); larger beets should be halved or quartered
6 heads garlic, halved horizontally (roast covered for 20 minutes, uncovered for 6 minutes)

Keep in mind that the vegetables need not be exotic, but they must be fresh. Once vegetables are harvested, they begin to lose their natural sugars. The longer they are in storage, the less desirable they are for this (or any) cooking method.

ASPARAGUS IN BED

This recipe is an adaptation of the *asparagi Bismarck* served at Bagutta, a wonderful old restaurant in Milan. There, the asparagus are steamed and topped with a fried egg. At Al Forno, we have adapted the idea to fit our cooking methods by roasting the asparagus. We then top them with the fried egg and a generous dusting of freshly grated Parmigiano-Reggiano. When the yolk is pierced, it combines with the cheese, creating its own sauce.

On our menu, we call this Asparagus in Bed because the egg covers the spears like a blanket, leaving just the tips poking out.

Serve Asparagus in Bed as an appetizer or as a light luncheon dish.

2 pounds asparagus, trimmed
3 tablespoons virgin olive oil
1/8 teaspoon kosher salt
2 tablespoons unsalted butter
4 eggs
1/2 cup freshly grated Parmigiano-Reggiano (1 1/2 ounces)

1. Preheat the oven to 500 degrees.

2. Spread the asparagus out on a baking sheet in a single layer and brush them with the olive oil. Sprinkle with salt and roast in the upper third of the oven until the spears are tender when pierced with the tip of a knife, about 10 to 12 minutes, depending on their thickness. While the asparagus are in the oven, begin frying the eggs so that they will be ready at the same time as the asparagus.

3. Melt the butter in a large skillet. Break the eggs into the pan and cook until the whites set and the yolks are still soft.

4. Remove the asparagus from the oven and divide them among 4 heated plates. With a spatula, place the eggs over the spears, leaving only the tips of the asparagus exposed, and top with the cheese. Drizzle the melted butter left in the skillet over the cheese and serve.

SERVES 4

TUSCAN BEAN PUREE

1 pound small navy beans, washed and picked over
1 cup virgin olive oil
4 fresh sage leaves (see note)
4 garlic cloves, peeled and trimmed
2 teaspoons kosher salt

1. Place the beans in a heavy stockpot with 7 cups of water, 3 tablespoons of olive oil, sage leaves, garlic cloves, and salt. Bring to a boil, reduce the heat, and simmer, uncovered, until the beans are very soft, about 1 hour, adding more water if necessary. The beans will cook down almost to a puree, and most of the water will be absorbed. Remove the sage leaves and allow the beans to cool for 10 minutes.

2. In a food processor fitted with the steel blade, puree the bean mixture, adding the remaining olive oil through the feed tube. Process until the consistency is smooth.

MAKES ABOUT 3 CUPS OF PUREE; SERVES 6 AS A SIDE DISH OR UP TO 20 AS PART OF AN ANTIPASTO

Note: If fresh sage is unavailable, do not use dried. You may substitute a sprig of fresh rosemary or 8 leaves of dried rosemary.

GRILLED CAPONATA

aponata is a Sicilian dish. It is typical of the style called *agrodolce,* or sweet and sour. The fact that the vegetables are grilled distinguishes this recipe from traditional caponata. Don't be alarmed by the inclusion of cocoa in the list below; it adds a depth of flavor, rich color, and a subtle, mysterious taste.

1/3 cup dried currants
1/2 cup yellow raisins
2 medium eggplant (3 pounds), cut into 5/8-inch-thick rounds
5 large onions (about 2 pounds), peeled and cut horizontally into
 5/8-inch-thick slices
1 cup virgin olive oil
1 tablespoon sifted unsweetened cocoa powder
1 1/4 cups chopped canned whole tomatoes in heavy puree
1 tablespoon capers in salt
15 pitted and sliced green olives
15 Kalamata olives, pitted and quartered
3/4 cup balsamic vinegar

1. Prepare a charcoal fire, placing the grill rack about 4 inches above the fire (see note).

2. Soak the currants and raisins in hot water to cover for 5 minutes; drain them and set aside.

3. Brush both sides of the eggplant and onion slices with about 1/4 cup of olive oil. Grill the eggplant slices for about 5 minutes per side, until they are lightly charred and soft inside. Grill the onion slices until lightly charred but cooked through, about 7 minutes per side. Transfer the vegetables to a cutting board. When cool enough to handle, coarsely chop them and set aside.

4. In a mixing bowl, fold the cocoa into the chopped tomatoes. Add all the remaining ingredients and toss to combine. The caponata

together. Repeat with the remaining eggplant slices, and place the sandwiches in an oiled, shallow baking dish in 1 layer. Pour half the tomatoes and their puree around the "sandwiches," and top the eggplant with the remainder.

7. Bake for 15 to 17 minutes, until the tomato is bubbling hot and the sandwiches are heated through.

MAKES 12 SANDWICHES FOR 12 VEGETABLE
ACCOMPANIMENTS OR 6 LIGHT MAIN COURSES

AL FORNO'S MASHED POTATOES

2 pounds small red potatoes, quartered, skins on
1/2 cup heavy cream
8 tablespoons (1 stick) unsalted butter, at room temperature
1 teaspoon kosher salt

1. Place the potatoes in a saucepan, adding enough water to cover them by 1 inch. Bring to a boil, lower the heat, and simmer until the potatoes are soft, about 15 minutes.

2. Drain the potatoes in a colander and return them to the saucepan. Over very low heat, coarsly mash the potatoes with an old-fashioned masher or 2 large forks, gradually adding the heavy cream and butter. Stir in the salt, up to 1 teaspoon, or just enough to suit your taste. Serve piping hot.

SERVES 6

CHARRED AND PEELED BELL PEPPERS

There are several ways to char and remove the skins from bell peppers. Roasting them over a hardwood charcoal fire is the best method because it imparts a mild, smoky flavor; however, you can achieve fine results in your kitchen over a gas flame or under your broiler. Place the peppers directly over the flame of a gas stovetop, or 4 inches from the element of an electric broiler. Turn and char the peppers as described in this recipe.

These peppers may be served as a simple vegetable accompaniment drizzled with olive oil, or you may use them as an ingredient for an antipasto or salad.

6 red or yellow bell peppers
3 tablespoons virgin olive oil
1/8 teaspoon kosher salt

1. Prepare a very hot hardwood charcoal fire, setting the grill rack about 3 to 4 inches above the coals. The fire must be very hot so the skins will blister and char without the flesh dehydrating.

2. Grill the peppers on one side until the skins char and blister. Rotate and continue to grill them until the skins are blackened on all sides.

3. Transfer the peppers to a covered plastic container where the steam will aid in separating the skin from the pulp. Set aside for about 10 minutes; then one by one, peel the charred skin from the pulp.

4. Place the peppers on a serving dish, drizzle with the olive oil, and sprinkle with salt. The peppers may be served at once, or in the Italian tradition—at room temperature—which allows you to appreciate their subtle flavors more fully.

SERVES 3 AS A FIRST COURSE
OR 6 AS A VEGETABLE ACCOMPANIMENT

GRILLED PEPPERS WITH ANCHOVY AND GARLIC

1/4 cup virgin olive oil
2 anchovy fillets, rinsed, patted dry, and finely chopped
1 teaspoon minced fresh garlic
6 red bell peppers, halved lengthwise and seeded
Six 5/8-inch-thick slices country bread
1 whole garlic clove, peeled
1/4 teaspoon kosher salt
1/4 cup chopped fresh Italian parsley
1 lemon, cut into 6 wedges

1. Prepare a charcoal fire, setting the grate 4 inches above the coals.

2. Combine the olive oil, anchovies, and garlic in a small bowl and stir to combine.

3. Brush the peppers, inside and out, with some of the flavored olive oil and place them on the grill cut side down. Grill them for about 8 minutes, until their cut edges have charred and the domes of the peppers give slightly under the pressure of a fingertip.

4. Transfer the peppers to a serving platter and place the bread slices on the grill. Toast both sides of the bread, remove the slices from the grill, and rub them with the whole garlic clove.

5. Cut the bread into small cubes or croutons, scatter them around the peppers, and top with the salt and the remaining olive oil.

6. Garnish with chopped parsley and lemon wedges. You may serve the peppers hot or at room temperature.

SERVES 6

GRILLED PEPPERS AGRODOLCE

*A*grodolce is a common cooking term in Italy. It means "sweet and sour." There are several recipes in this book using this balance of flavors. These dishes are generally found in southern Italy, but the Venetians have a great variety of sweet-and-sour recipes as well. For instance, they marinate fried sole fillets in vinegar with raisins, bay leaves, pine nuts, cloves, and ground cinnamon. For their liver *agrodolce,* they make a simple sauce by combining lemon juice and sugar.

For these peppers, we use balsamic vinegar and raisins. The balsamic vinegar has a rich, mellow taste that is both sweet and sharp.

2 tablespoons golden raisins
3 red or yellow bell peppers, halved lengthwise and seeded
1/2 cup virgin olive oil
1/3 cup balsamic vinegar
1/2 teaspoon minced garlic
1/2 teaspoon kosher salt

1. Prepare a charcoal fire, placing the grill rack about 3 inches above the coals (see note).

2. Soften the raisins in hot water to cover for 5 minutes. Drain and set aside.

3. Brush the inside of the pepper halves with 1 tablespoon of olive oil and place them cut side down on the grill. Grill for about 8 minutes, until the cut edges begin to char and the domes of the peppers give slightly under the pressure of a fingertip.

4. Remove the peppers from the grill and stack them one on top of another in a small bowl. This will produce enough steam to continue to cook and soften the peppers. Set aside for 15 minutes.

5. Cut the peppers into thin strips. Combine them in a mixing bowl with the raisins, the remaining olive oil, balsamic vinegar, garlic, and salt. Toss, and allow the peppers to marinate at room temperature

for at least 30 minutes before serving. These peppers may be prepared up to 3 days in advance and refrigerated; however, they are best served at room temperature and should be removed from the refrigerator about 1 hour before serving.

SERVES 6

Note: Grilling the peppers in this manner keeps their skins intact. If you cannot grill them, a good alternative is to remove their skins completely by following the instructions for charring and peeling peppers over a gas flame or electric broiler on page 150. Cut the peeled peppers in half lengthwise, remove their seeds, and proceed with step 5 of this recipe.

CAVOLO E PANCETTA SOPPRESA

I f you are not a cabbage lover, this recipe could change your mind. It is very easy to prepare and can be served as an appetizer or as an accompaniment to simple grilled chicken or sausages.

7 cups finely shredded savoy cabbage (1 head)
1 cup heavy cream
1/4 cup freshly grated Pecorino Romano
1/4 cup shredded Bel Paese or fontina
1/4 cup crumbled Gorgonzola
1/4 teaspoon crushed red pepper flakes
2 ounces pancetta, chopped (1/4 cup packed)

1. Preheat the oven to 500 degrees.

2. Combine all the ingredients except the pancetta in a mixing bowl, toss them to combine, and transfer to a shallow ceramic baking dish (6- to 8-cup capacity; see note).

3. Top the cabbage with the pancetta and bake for 15 to 18 minutes. The cabbage will be cooked through and crusty on top. The sauce should be thick and creamy and the pancetta nicely browned.

SERVES 4 TO 6

Note: Use a ceramic dish rather than a metal one. Metal conducts heat quickly, and it could cause the cabbage to burn around the edges.

Roasted Onions Agrodolce

5 large red onions (2 pounds)
1/3 cup plus 1 tablespoon virgin olive oil
1/2 cup balsamic vinegar
1 teaspoon kosher salt

1. Preheat the oven to 450 degrees.

2. Slice the tops off the onions and peel them, keeping the root ends intact.

3. Place the onion wedges cut side down on a board. Slice them in half vertically through the root. Cut each half into 4 wedges, taking care to cut each piece through the root, which will keep the wedges intact.

4. Place the onions in one layer in a 9 × 12-inch baking dish. Brush them with the olive oil, drizzle with balsamic vinegar, sprinkle with salt, and cover with foil.

5. Bake the onions for 45 minutes, uncover, and bake for an additional 5 minutes until they are soft and the juices have caramelized.

SERVES 6 AS A VEGETABLE ACCOMPANIMENT
OR 12 AS PART OF AN ANTIPASTO

SWEET-CORN FRITTERS

The taste of fresh corn is very delicate and sweet. Its natural sugar turns into starch soon after it is picked, however. We make these fritters in the summer when we can buy Silver Queen, a delicious white corn, from Coll Walker's farm. These fritters need no other seasoning; the flavor of fresh corn cannot be improved.

3 ears fresh sweet corn, preferably Silver Queen
1¼ cups unbleached flour
2 teaspoons baking powder
1 tablespoon sugar
2 eggs
2/3 cup milk
1/2 teaspoon cayenne
2 teaspoons kosher salt
Peanut oil for deep frying

1. Bring a pot of salted water to a boil. Husk the corn, drop it into the boiling water, and cook for 3 minutes. Drain the corn and refresh it under cold running water.

2. Drain the corn and cut off the kernels (you will have about 1½ cups). Set aside.

3. Sift the flour, baking powder, and sugar into a mixing bowl. Whisk the eggs together with the milk, cayenne, and salt, and add to the dry ingredients in the mixing bowl. Mix well and fold the corn into the batter. Chill for 1 hour.

4. Heat the oil to 375 degrees in a deep fryer. Drop the batter by tablespoons into the hot oil, being careful not to crowd the pot. Cook

the fritters, turning once, until they are brown, 2 to 3 minutes per side. Drain on paper towels and serve piping hot.

MAKES ABOUT 24 FRITTERS OR ENOUGH
FOR 6 TO 8 APPETIZERS OR SIDE PLATES

Note: These fritters are just fine on their own with no accompaniment. However, if you enjoy hot-and-sweet flavor combinations, as we do, you can serve them with a mayonnaise flavored with West Indian hot sauce.

BRAISED AND SPICED SPLIT PEAS

3 tablespoons virgin olive oil
3 ounces pancetta, chopped (1/2 cup packed)
1 cup chopped onion
3 carrots, scraped and chopped
1 stalk celery, chopped
1 pound split peas
1/4 teaspoon cayenne
7 cups boiling water
1/2 teaspoon kosher salt
1 teaspoon minced fresh ginger

1. Heat the olive oil in a large, heavy saucepan. Add the pancetta and sauté until it begins to brown, about 5 minutes. Add the onion, carrot, and celery, and sauté for an additional 5 to 7 minutes, stirring the vegetables with a wooden spoon to loosen any browned bits from the pancetta. At this point, the onion will have softened and become translucent.

2. Add the split peas and cayenne to the sautéed vegetables, cover with the boiling water, and simmer over low heat until the peas are very soft and the consistency is thick, with most of the water evaporated, about 1 hour. Watch the peas carefully, stirring often in the last 15 minutes of cooking time. As the peas break apart, they create a thick, chunky puree that can easily burn.

3. Add the salt and minced ginger, stirring to combine. Serve immediately.

SERVES 8 TO 12

SAUTÉED RAPINI WITH RAISINS AND GARLIC

apini, or broccoli di rape, is a bitter Italian green. It can be found in Italian markets or well-stocked supermarkets.

2 pounds rapini, washed, trimmed, and chopped
6 tablespoons virgin olive oil
2 teaspoons minced fresh garlic
1/2 cup raisins
3/4 teaspoon kosher salt
1/2 teaspoon crushed red pepper flakes

1. Bring 4 quarts of water to a boil in a large pot. Drop in the rapini and blanch for 7 minutes. Drain the rapini in a colander, run cold water over to refresh it, and set aside.

2. Heat 4 tablespoons of olive oil in a large skillet. Add the garlic and sauté until golden. Add the blanched rapini, raisins, salt, and pepper. Sauté for 7 to 10 minutes, until the rapini is heated through. Drizzle with the remaining olive oil and serve hot or at room temperature.

SERVES 4 TO 6

CHUTNEYS,
CONDIMENTS,
AND RELISHES

George and I love condiments. We like the surprise, extra flavor, and the punch that a chutney or relish gives to a simple grilled dish. We play with flavor balances by using condiments. And we like the sensation of several different tastes on a plate that a selection of chutneys provides.

George's favorite combination is hot/sweet, and there are plenty of examples of it in this chapter. I like a more subtle use of sweet and often use balsamic vinegar for the sweet, complex flavor it lends to condiments, as in the caramelized garlic. All of these recipes are easy to prepare and most require very little time—usually less than 1/2 hour. Sometimes, they can be spur-of-the-moment preparations when you find yourself with an overabundance of ripe fruit or vegetables from the garden. They make great garnishes and taste tinglers.

Clockwise, from top: Grilled Chicken Paillards with Lemon Aspic and Sultanas (page 128) and Caramelized Cranberry-Apple Chutney (page 176); Grilled Delmonico Steak with Two Homemade Catsups (page 122); and Spicy Cantaloupe Chutney (page 175).

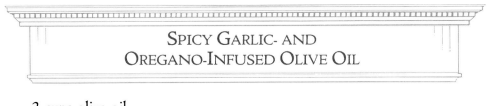

INFUSED OILS

We infuse, or flavor, olive oil with a number of different ingredients. We use these oils to dress salads, or we drizzle them over grilled meats, pasta, and pizzas. They are very easy to make and add a new dimension to simple foods. Most of them will keep for at least 2 weeks in the refrigerator. If you start with an unopened bottle of oil, these infusions will keep refrigerated for a month or two. These recipes can easily be halved.

SPICY GARLIC- AND OREGANO-INFUSED OLIVE OIL

2 cups olive oil
8 garlic cloves, peeled and trimmed
2 tablespoons dried oregano
2 teaspoons crushed red pepper flakes

Follow the instructions for Hot Pepper–Infused Olive Oil (page 166) using the above ingredients. This oil is especially good drizzled on Grilled Pizza Margarita (page 80).

MAKES 2 CUPS

FENNEL OIL

2½ cups chopped fresh fennel (1¼ pounds)
2 cups olive oil
1½ teaspoons fennel seed

1. Combine the fresh fennel and olive oil in a heavy saucepan. Slowly bring the oil to a boil, then reduce the heat to the barest simmer. A heat diffuser on your burner would be useful here. Allow the mixture to simmer until the fennel is very soft and almost melting into the oil, about 45 minutes.

2. Add the fennel seed and simmer for another 10 minutes.

3. Remove the oil from the heat and set aside for 30 minutes to allow the fennel seed to infuse the oil.

4. When the oil is at room temperature, strain it into a clean jar, pressing gently on the solids to extract as much flavor as possible. Refrigerate the oil, covered, for up to 1 week. Transfer the fennel in the strainer to another container. It will make a tasty topping for bruschetta.

MAKES 2 CUPS

SPICY GARLIC- AND FENNEL-INFUSED OLIVE OIL

2 cups olive oil
1/3 cup Chinese crushed red pepper (see note)
1 tablespoon ground black pepper
1/8 cup fennel seed
2 garlic cloves, peeled and trimmed

Follow exactly the instructions for Hot Pepper–Infused Olive Oil (page 166), substituting the peppers, fennel seeds, and garlic.

MAKES 2 CUPS

Note: This is a ground version of those small, red, fiery hot dried chile peppers.

TOMATO OIL

This is good to make at the end of the summer when you have lots of ripe garden tomatoes on your hands.

2 pounds fresh tomatoes, peeled, halved, and seeded
10 garlic cloves, peeled and trimmed
3 jalapeño peppers, sliced
3 cups olive oil

1. Combine all the ingredients in a heavy saucepan. Bring to a boil, then reduce the heat to the barest simmer. Allow the oil to simmer for 1 hour, until the garlic and tomatoes are very soft. Remove from the heat and set aside to cool.

2. When the oil is at room temperature, strain it into a clean jar, cover, and refrigerate for up to 1 week. Transfer the tomatoes and solids into another container and reserve to spread on bruschetta.

MAKES 3 CUPS

HOT PEPPER-INFUSED OLIVE OIL

3 cups olive oil
1/4 cup hot Hungarian paprika
1/4 cup crushed red pepper flakes
3 garlic cloves, peeled and trimmed

1. Combine all the ingredients in a heavy saucepan. Bring to a boil, lower the heat to very low, and gently simmer for 10 minutes. Remove from the heat and set aside for 30 minutes so the flavors continue to infuse the oil as it cools.

2. Strain the oil into a clean jar. When it has cooled to room temperature, cover and refrigerate until ready to use. The oil will keep in the refrigerator for at least 2 weeks.

MAKES ABOUT 3 CUPS

Caramelized Garlic

This is a garlic lover's dream. A friend calls this "garlic candy." Serve these little morsels on an antipasto platter or with grilled meats or chicken, or combine them with olive oil to dress pasta.

1½ cups peeled and trimmed garlic cloves (see note)
1¼ cups balsamic vinegar
3 tablespoons olive oil

Combine all the ingredients in a heavy saucepan that accommodates the garlic in one layer. Bring the liquid to a boil, reduce the heat to very low, and simmer gently until the garlic cloves are very soft and the balsamic vinegar has become thick and syrupy, about 30 to 40 minutes. Set aside to cool. This will keep refrigerated for at least a week.

MAKES 1 GENEROUS CUP, OR 8 ANTIPASTO PORTIONS

Note: Peeling this much garlic can be tedious and time consuming. Our secret for easy peeling is to separate the cloves, slice off the root end, and refrigerate overnight. The skins almost pop off.

WINTER RELISH

This relish can be used as an accompaniment to grilled chicken, sausages, or pork chops. It is also a great topping for bruschetta or buttered slices of good country bread.

1 onion, chopped
4 stalks celery, chopped
1 jalapeño pepper, seeded and chopped
1/2 teaspoon hot sauce
3/4 cup chopped green olives
1/4 cup virgin olive oil
2 tablespoons red-wine vinegar

Combine all the ingredients in a small mixing bowl. Cover and chill until ready to use. This relish will keep well overnight.

MAKES 1½ TO 2 CUPS

SPICED OLIVES

This is one of the condiments we use on our antipasto platter. On their own, these olives are a welcome tidbit to serve with an *aperitivo* or cocktail. They also make a nice addition to salads.

2 cups Kalamata or oil-cured olives
2 teaspoons crushed red pepper flakes
1 teaspoon ground cumin
Zest and juice of 1 lemon
1/2 cup olive oil
1/2 teaspoon minced fresh garlic (optional)

Combine all the ingredients in a bowl. Marinate at room temperature for 1 hour so that the flavors can marry, or store in a covered container in the refrigerator until ready to use. Without the fresh garlic, they will keep almost indefinitely. You can, if you choose, add garlic just before serving. With the garlic these olives will keep for up to a week.

MAKES 2 CUPS

BLACK- OR GREEN-OLIVE PUREE

This puree is best made with good-quality olives. Kalamata olives, oil-cured olives, or green Sicilian or Greek olives are best. We do not recommend canned pitted olives.

Use the puree on bruschetta and pizzas, in pastas, or just spread on buttered bread for an appetizer.

1 cup pitted black or green olives
1/2 cup virgin olive oil

Combine the olives and oil in a food processor. Puree. Transfer to a container, cover, and refrigerate until ready to use. This will keep well in the refrigerator overnight. It will keep up to 1 week if the surface of the puree is covered with additional olive oil.

MAKES 1 CUP

SPICY TOMATO CATSUP

The next two recipes are components of an Al Forno signature dish, Grilled Delmonico Steak with Two Homemade Catsups (page 122). The catsups are equally delicious on a basic burger or chicken sandwich, or wherever you enjoy a catsup fix.

1/2 cup sugar
3/4 cup chopped onion
1 tablespoon minced fresh garlic
1 red bell pepper, halved, seeded, and chopped
6 cups chopped canned tomatoes in heavy puree
3/4 cup red-wine vinegar
1/4 cup balsamic vinegar
1 to 2 teaspoons cayenne

1. Caramelize the sugar in a heavy saucepan over medium heat by stirring it constantly until it melts and gradually turns a rich mahogany color, 5 to 10 minutes.

2. Add the onion, garlic, and bell pepper. Cook for 5 minutes. Add all the remaining ingredients except the cayenne, and bring to a boil.

3. Reduce the heat to very low, and simmer, stirring occasionally, until the mixture thickens, about 45 minutes. Puree and add cayenne to taste. Cool to room temperature, transfer to a covered container, and refrigerate for up to 2 weeks.

MAKES ABOUT 3½ CUPS

SPICY YELLOW-PEPPER CATSUP

8 large yellow bell peppers, halved and seeded (see note)
3 to 4 red jalapeño or other hot red peppers
2 tablespoons minced fresh garlic
3/4 cup red-wine vinegar
3/4 cup sugar
2 large onions (about 6 ounces), peeled and coarsely chopped

1. Coarsely puree the bell and hot peppers in a food processor.

2. Combine the pepper puree with the remaining ingredients in a heavy saucepan. Bring the mixture to a boil, and simmer over low heat 45 minutes to 1 hour, stirring often, until the vegetables are very soft.

3. Puree the mixture in a blender until it is very smooth. Cool and refrigerate until ready to use, or up to 1 week.

MAKES ABOUT 2 CUPS

Note: If yellow peppers are unavailable, substitute red.

HONEYED ONIONS

This is a great condiment to roast and serve with sole fillets or chicken. In cooking, the honey caramelizes, adding depth to the flavor of the onions.

1 cup red-wine vinegar
3/4 cup honey
4 large onions (about 1¼ pounds)

1. Combine the vinegar and honey in a mixing bowl. Stir until the honey is completely dissolved.

2. Peel the onions and cut them crosswise into paper-thin slices. Add the onions to the mixing bowl, separating the slices as you toss them in the liquid.

3. Allow the onions to marinate, tossing occasionally, for about 1 hour. This will keep, covered, in the refrigerator for 1 week.

MAKES ABOUT 3 CUPS

OVEN-CURED TOMATOES

This is good to make when tomatoes are at their peak. The cooking process dries the outside of the tomato, concentrates its natural sugars, and leaves the inner pulp soft and juicy.

Keep in mind the recipe requires twelve hours' cooking time so plan ahead. You can roast the tomatoes overnight if your oven is dependable and keeps a constant temperature.

We use these tomatoes as an ingredient in salads (see Spicy Clam Salad on page 47) and relishes, but they are also a wonderful accompaniment to grilled meats.

12 medium garden tomatoes, cored
12 leaves fresh basil or parsley, or 12 thyme branches
1/4 cup virgin olive oil

1. Preheat the oven to 200 degrees.

2. Stuff the cavities of the cored tomatoes with the herb of your choice.

3. Place the tomatoes in a baking dish just large enough to hold them in 1 layer. Drizzle with olive oil and bake for 8 to 12 hours. The skins should shrivel and dry, but the insides should remain soft and juicy. As a condiment, you can serve the tomatoes hot or cold. They will keep in the refrigerator for 4 to 5 days.

**SERVES 12 AS A CONDIMENT
OR 6 AS A VEGETABLE ACCOMPANIMENT**

VARIATION: This recipe works equally well with cherry tomatoes. Place them in a baking dish in one layer, drizzle with olive oil, and scatter herbs around them. Reduce the baking time to 2 to 4 hours.

SWEET-AND-SOUR PRUNES

We like to serve this condiment with grilled or roasted pork.

1 pound pitted prunes
3/4 cup sugar
6 tablespoons sherry vinegar

1. Combine the prunes, sugar, and 3 cups of water in a saucepan. Bring to a boil, lower the heat, and simmer until the prunes are soft and the liquid syrupy, about 15 minutes.

2. Remove from the heat and stir in the vinegar. Serve hot or cold. The prunes will keep, refrigerated, for 1 week.

MAKES 1½ TO 2 CUPS

DESSERTS

I took charge of desserts at the restaurant by default. That responsibility happened to fall into my lap as other responsibilities fell naturally to George. Our dessert recipes, like all our ideas, develop through our combined inspirations, as well as from staff members who have come and gone. The priority has always been to create desserts with the same integrity as the rest of our food. We weren't interested in producing conventional sweets; we wanted to offer something special. Over the years, our repertoire has grown enormously as we put greater demands on ourselves and our staff. At this point, all desserts but one or two are made to order. There is nothing worse than a soggy piece of pastry, or one that tastes of the refrigerator. And there is nothing more satisfying than a warm *crostata*, or tart, a miniature cake hot from the oven, a fruit gratin bursting with flavor, or ice cream churned just for you. These are the kind of indulgences we love to provide for our customers and friends.

This chapter represents a small selection of our desserts. The recipes could have gone on forever, but our editor finally said ENOUGH! You will be able to multiply the number of recipes we give with variations of your own. Use your favorite fruits in the crostata or gratin. In spring, fill the crostata with thinly sliced rhubarb and strawberries—it's incredible. In winter, spread the butter crust with a puree of dates topped with pecan halves and cinnamon-sugar—a great combination. The ingredients need not be complex or exotic to create a fabulous dessert. Can you think of anything more wonderful than filling your kitchen with the aroma of fresh fruit baking on a butter crust, or the bittersweet smell of pears roasting in a dark caramel with rich Mascarpone custard?

Caramelized Pumpkin Crostata (page 188).

CROSTATAS

The rustic crostata makes a lovely end to a meal. It is a tart made freeform, rather than in a conventional fluted tart pan, giving us crust lovers more area of thin, flaky pastry to enjoy.

The following recipes are easy to prepare, and several steps can be done ahead. You can roll the dough and lay it out on a baking sheet a few hours before serving. Be sure to keep it well wrapped and refrigerated if you do so. You can even assemble the tart if you are using berries or a fruit that won't weep or darken. Otherwise, have all the ingredients prepared and ready to use. Remember to remove the rolled tart dough from the refrigerator 5 minutes before assembling so it will be pliable enough to fold over the filling without cracking. Do not keep the unbaked tart at room temperature any longer than necessary to assemble. The butter content in the dough is high, and to ensure a flaky crust it should go into the oven while still cold.

FOOD-PROCESSOR TART DOUGH

1/2 pound (2 sticks) cold unsalted butter
2 cups unbleached flour
1/4 cup superfine sugar
1/2 teaspoon kosher salt
1/4 cup ice water

1. This recipe works best with very cold butter. Cut the butter into 1/2-inch cubes. Since butter softens rapidly with handling, return the cubes to the refrigerator for at least 10 minutes while you set up the food processor and gather the dry ingredients.

2. Place the flour, sugar, and salt in the bowl of a food processor fitted with the steel blade. Pulse a few times to combine.

3. Add the butter, tossing quickly with your fingers to coat each

cube with flour, taking care not to touch the blade. This prevents the butter cubes from adhering together and helps them to break apart and combine more evenly with the flour.

4. Pulse 15 times, or until the butter particles are the size of small peas.

5. With the motor running, add the ice water all at once through the feed tube. Process for about 10 seconds, stopping the machine before the dough becomes a solid mass.

6. Turn the contents of the bowl onto a sheet of aluminum foil, pressing any loose particles into the mass of dough. Roughly form the dough into a 7-inch disk.

7. Cover the dough completely with aluminum foil and refrigerate for at least 1 hour. The dough may be refrigerated up to 2 days or frozen for up to 2 weeks (see note).

MAKES 18 TO 20 OUNCES OF DOUGH,
OR ENOUGH FOR ONE LARGE TART,
TWO 9-INCH SHELLS, OR FOUR LITTLE TARTS FOR 2

Note: This tart dough freezes well for up to 2 weeks. It is one of the few things I keep in my freezer at home, for unexpected gatherings or last-minute desserts. For convenience, wrap the dough in the portion size you are most likely to use. If it is frozen, defrost the dough, wrapped, on your counter for 30 to 45 minutes or until it is still quite cold but pliable.

9 to 10 ounces Food-Processor Tart Dough (page 182)
Flour for dusting
2 tablespoons plus 2 teaspoons superfine sugar
2 cups fresh raspberries
Confectioners' sugar for dusting

1. Preheat the oven to 450 degrees.

2. Roll the dough on a lightly floured surface to an 11-inch free-form circle. Transfer to a baking sheet and sprinkle with 1 tablespoon superfine sugar.

3. Leaving a 1½-inch border all around, cover the dough with the raspberries, stem ends down. Starting in the center, work your way toward the outside in concentric circles. Most of the berries will fit on the shell in one layer; mound any extra berries in the center. Sprinkle the berries with the remaining superfine sugar.

4. Raise the dough border to enclose the sides of the tart, letting it drape gently over the fruit. Press down on the dough at the baking sheet, snugly securing the sides and the bottom of the pastry; be careful not to mash the fruit. Gently pinch the soft pleats that form from the draping.

5. Bake the tart for 20 to 25 minutes, until the fruit has given off some of its juice and the dough is golden.

6. Cool on a rack for about 10 minutes, dust with confectioners' sugar, and serve while still warm and aromatic.

SERVES 6 TO 8

BLACK MISSION FIG CROSTATA

2 tablespoons plus 1 teaspoon superfine sugar
1/4 teaspoon ground cinnamon
12 fresh black mission figs (about 12 ounces)
10 ounces Food-Processor Tart Dough (page 182)
Flour for dusting
Confectioners' sugar for dusting

1. Preheat the oven to 450 degrees.

2. Combine the superfine sugar and the cinnamon.

3. Remove the stems from the figs and cut them vertically into 1/4-inch-thick slices.

4. Roll the dough on a lightly floured surface into an 11-inch free-form circle. Transfer the dough to a baking sheet and sprinkle with 1 tablespoon of the cinnamon-sugar.

5. Starting in the center, cover the dough with overlapping fig slices in concentric circles, leaving a 1½-inch border on the outside. Sprinkle with the remaining cinnamon-sugar.

6. Raise the dough border to enclose the sides of the tart, letting it drape gently over the fruit. Press down on the dough at the baking sheet, snugly securing the sides and the bottom; be careful not to mash the fruit. Gently pinch the soft pleats that form from the draping.

7. Bake the tart for 20 to 25 minutes, until the crust is golden and the figs are soft and lightly caramelized.

8. Cool the tart on a rack for about 10 minutes. Dust with confectioners' sugar and serve warm.

SERVES 6 TO 8

10 ounces Food-Processor Tart Dough (page 182)
Flour for dusting
2 cups cranberries, washed and picked over
1/2 cup chopped walnuts
2 tablespoons superfine sugar
2 tablespoons packed dark brown sugar
Confectioners' sugar for dusting

1. Preheat the oven to 450 degrees.

2. Roll the tart dough into an 11-inch circle on a lightly floured surface, and transfer it to a baking sheet.

3. Combine the cranberries, walnuts, superfine sugar, and brown sugar in a mixing bowl. Toss to distribute the sugars evenly.

4. Cover the tart shell with the cranberry mixture, leaving a 1½-inch border around the outside edge.

5. Raise the dough border to enclose the sides of the tart, letting it drape gently over the fruit. Press down on the dough at the baking sheet, snugly securing the sides and the bottom; be careful not to mash the fruit. Gently pinch the soft pleats that form from the draping.

6. Bake the tart for 15 to 18 minutes, until the crust is golden and the berries are juicy. Cool on a rack for about 10 minutes, dust with confectioners' sugar, and serve warm with a pitcher of Nanci Courtney's Crème Anglaise (page 210) or whipped cream.

SERVES 6 TO 8

APPLE-CRISP CROSTATA

10 ounces Food-Processor Tart Dough (page 182)
1/4 cup unbleached flour
1/4 cup superfine sugar
4 tablespoons (1/2 stick) cold unsalted butter
1½ pounds (about 3 large) McIntosh, Macoun, or Empire apples

1. Preheat the oven to 450 degrees.

2. Roll the tart dough into an 11-inch circle on a lightly floured surface, and transfer it to a baking sheet.

3. Combine the flour and sugar in a mixing bowl. With 2 knives, or with your fingertips, blend in the butter until the mixture crumbles and holds together in irregular lumps.

4. Peel, core, and quarter the apples. Cut each quarter into 3 chunks. Cover the tart dough with the apple chunks, leaving a 1½-inch border around the outside edge.

5. Cover the apples with the butter mixture, and raise the dough border to enclose the sides of the tart, letting it drape gently over the fruit. Press down on the dough at the baking sheet, snugly securing the sides and the bottom; be careful not to mash the fruit. Gently pinch the soft pleats that form from the draping.

6. Bake the tart for about 20 minutes, until the crust is golden and the apples are soft. Check the tart after 12 minutes; if the topping is browning too quickly, place a sheet of foil loosely over the top of the tart for the remainder of the baking time.

7. Cool the tart on a rack for about 10 minutes and serve warm.

SERVES 6 TO 8

CARAMELIZED PUMPKIN CROSTATA

Every year Coll Walker plants one of his fields with pumpkins for our restaurants. We set aside a Sunday morning, and with a group of friends we pick the pumpkins and transport them to Providence. One year we filled three pick-up trucks with about 350 pumpkins.

Besides appreciating the pumpkins for their looks, we love to cook with them. At Lucky's, we top one of our grilled pizzas with dollops of pumpkin puree, we stuff cabbage leaves with pumpkin and butternut squash, and we make miniature cakes with pumpkin. At Al Forno, we fill pasta with pumpkin, we flavor our Bolognese sauce with pumpkin, and this year we have a new pumpkin dessert.

This is a different approach to pumpkin pie. The traditional pumpkin-custard tart would not do, so we decided to separate the components, eliminate the predictable spices, and bake the tart to order. The crostata is assembled and baked while the customer is eating the main course. The warm tart goes to the table in a generous pool of crème anglaise, accompanied by a drizzle of caramel sauce and a dollop of whipped cream.

1 small sugar pumpkin (4 pounds)
2 tablespoons unsalted butter
1 cup sugar
18 to 20 ounces Food-Processor Tart Dough (page 182)
1 cup heavy cream
Caramel Sauce (page 213)
Nanci Courtney's Crème Anglaise (page 210)
Confectioners' sugar for dusting

1. Preheat the oven to 500 degrees.

2. Cut the pumpkin in half, scoop out the seeds, and place the halves, cut sides down, on a baking sheet.

3. Roast the pumpkin until the flesh is very soft, about 20 to 25 minutes. Remove the pumpkin from the oven and allow it to cool until you can handle it. Turn the oven off.

4. Scoop the flesh from the pumpkin shells and set aside.

5. Melt the butter in a heavy skillet large enough to accommodate the pumpkin pulp. Add the sugar and stir constantly over low heat until the sugar caramelizes and becomes a rich mahogany brown.

6. Add the pumpkin, being careful not to burn yourself as the caramel may spatter. Toss the pumpkin in the caramel to coat it. The caramel may seize or solidify, but it will melt again after a few minutes as the pulp heats in the pan. When the pulp is well combined with the caramel, transfer it to a bowl and set the mixture aside in the refrigerator to chill completely, at least 1 hour.

7. Preheat the oven to 450 degrees.

8. Roll out the dough into a 13- to 15-inch circle or rectangle on a floured surface and transfer it to a baking sheet. Top with the caramelized pumpkin, leaving a 2-inch border all around the outside of the dough.

9. Raise the dough border to enclose the sides of the tart, letting it drape gently over the fruit. Press down on the dough at the baking sheet, snugly securing the sides and the bottom; be careful not to mash the fruit. Gently pinch the soft pleats that form from the draping.

10. Bake the tart for about 18 to 22 minutes, until the crust is golden.

11. Whip the cream until stiff.

12. Serve the tart warm dusted with confectioners' sugar on a pool of crème anglaise. Pass a small pitcher of warm caramel sauce and the bowl of whipped cream.

SERVES 12

MASCARPONE CUSTARD

Fresh fruit gratins made with this Mascarpone custard are so luscious that they have inspired an X-rated comment from one prominent critic. The Mascarpone adds a wonderful richness and makes the gratin decidedly Italian in spirit. The technique for all the gratins that follow is basically the same.

1 cup milk
2 egg yolks
1/2 cup sugar
1/4 cup unbleached flour
3/4 cup heavy cream
1 teaspoon pure vanilla extract
1/2 cup Mascarpone

1. Scald the milk in a heavy saucepan.

2. In a bowl, beat the egg yolks until they are light and pale in color. Add the sugar, tablespoon by tablespoon, beating well after each addition. Fold in the flour and beat until smooth.

3. Pour the hot milk into the yolk mixture in a slow stream, beating constantly until smooth. Return the mixture to the saucepan and cook, stirring, until the mixture comes to a boil. Boil for 2 minutes, remove from heat, and transfer to a mixing bowl to cool to room temperature. Refrigerate the mixture, covered, for at least 1 hour, until well chilled.

4. To finish the custard, whip the cream with the vanilla until it thickens and begins to hold its shape.

5. Whisk the chilled yolk mixture until smooth. Fold the Mascarpone into the yolk mixture and gently fold in the whipped cream. Chill until ready to use or for up to 2 days.

MAKES 3 CUPS OR ENOUGH FOR 6 TO 8 GRATINS

RED-RASPBERRY GRATIN

3 cups Mascarpone Custard (page 190)
4½ cups fresh raspberries
3 teaspoons confectioners' sugar

1. Preheat the oven to 425 degrees. Position one rack in the middle of the oven and another about 4 inches below the broiler.

2. Lay out 6 individual, shallow, ceramic gratin dishes (1-cup capacity) on a baking sheet for easy handling.

3. Put 1/4 cup of Mascarpone Custard into each gratin dish. Divide the raspberries among them, sift 2 teaspoons of confectioners' sugar over the berries, and top them with the remaining custard. Sift 1 teaspoon of confectioners' sugar over the tops and bake on the middle rack of the oven for 5 to 7 minutes, until the custard is heated through and the berries have given off some of their juice.

4. Remove the gratins from the oven and change the setting to broil.

5. Place the gratins under the broiler and brown the custard for 1 to 1½ minutes, watching carefully to make sure the gratins don't burn. Serve immediately.

SERVES 6

VARIATION: This gratin is also delicious made with golden raspberries or a combination of red and golden.

You may also substitute blackberries. If you do so, increase the amount of confectioners' sugar to 9 teaspoons: 6 teaspoons for the blackberries and 3 teaspoons for the custard.

Pear "Tatin" Gratin

2 tablespoons unsalted butter
1/2 cup sugar
8 pears, peeled, halved lengthwise, cores removed
2 teaspoons minced candied ginger (optional)
3 cups Mascarpone Custard (page 190)

1. Preheat the oven to 450 degrees, positioning one rack in the middle of the oven and a second rack about 4 inches below the broiler.

2. To make the caramel, melt the butter in a large cast-iron skillet over medium heat. Add the sugar and stir constantly with a wooden spoon. Do not use a metal spoon as the high heat produced from the sugar will be conducted through the spoon, making it too hot to hold. The sugar will slowly melt into the butter. Lower the heat and keep stirring while the butter and sugar gradually darken to a rich mahogany color. This can take 10 to 15 minutes over a low flame. Immediately remove the skillet from the heat and continue to stir for a few minutes to stop the cooking and to cool the mixture. The caramel will continue to darken so it is important to remove it from the heat when it is one shade lighter than you want it. Don't worry if the sugar lumps a bit during the cooking process. Break up the lumps with the wooden spoon and they will melt and be incorporated as the caramel darkens. Also, if you do not proceed immediately with the recipe, the caramel may solidify and the butter may separate. Don't be alarmed; this is normal. The caramel will melt again as heat is applied.

3. Arrange the pear halves, cut sides down, on top of the caramel, being careful not to burn yourself, as the caramel may spatter if it is still hot. Scatter the minced ginger over the pears, cover with foil, and bake until the pears are soft, about 20 minutes for ripe pears and about 45 minutes for hard ones. The recipe may be completed to this point up to 2 days in advance. Cool the pears to room temperature, cover, and refrigerate until 1 hour before serving time.

4. To bake the gratins, place 1 heaping tablespoon of Mascarpone Custard in 8 individual, shallow, ceramic gratin dishes (1-cup capacity). Top the custard with 2 pear halves each, 1 to 2 tablespoons of the caramel, and an additional 2 to 3 tablespoons of Mascarpone Custard to cover the pears.

5. Place the gratin dishes on a baking sheet for easy handling and bake for 5 to 7 minutes, until the custard is heated through. Remove from the oven.

6. Change the oven setting to broil and brown the gratins for about 1 to 1½ minutes, watching carefully to make sure the custard doesn't burn. Serve immediately.

SERVES 8

RHODE ISLAND SHORTCAKES
WITH FRESH STRAWBERRIES

We make our shortcake biscuits with johnnycake meal, a fine white cornmeal made from Narragansett Indian corn. It is stone-ground at Gray's Grist Mill in Adamsville, Rhode Island. The cornmeal adds a unique flavor and texture to the biscuits. The ginger enhances the taste of the fruit. Look for ripe, juicy, fragrant berries.

SHORTCAKE BISCUITS

1½ cups unbleached flour
1/2 cup stone-ground white cornmeal (see note)
3 tablespoons sugar
4 teaspoons baking powder
4 tablespoons (1/2 stick) cold unsalted butter, cut into 12 pieces
1 teaspoon minced fresh ginger (optional)
1¼ cups heavy cream
Flour for dusting the dough

ASSEMBLY

2 cups heavy cream
1 teaspoon pure vanilla extract
1 quart fresh strawberries, hulled and sliced
2 to 3 tablespoons confectioners' sugar

1. Preheat the oven to 425 degrees and lightly butter a baking sheet.

2. Combine the flour, cornmeal, sugar, and baking powder in the bowl of a food processor fitted with the steel blade. Pulse a few times.

3. Add the butter and ginger and pulse 18 to 20 times, until the mixture resembles coarse meal.

4. Transfer the dry ingredients to a mixing bowl, making a well in the center. Pour 1 cup of heavy cream into the well and quickly

stir in the dry ingredients with a fork to form a mass. If the mixture seems too dry and does not hold together, add more heavy cream, a tablespoon at a time (up to 1/4 cup).

5. Turn the dough onto a pastry board and knead a few times to incorporate any dry particles; then, gently pat the dough into a rectangle 1¼ inches thick.

6. Cut the dough into 6 to 8 squares or rounds and place them on the baking sheet. Bake the shortcakes for 12 to 14 minutes, until they are golden.

7. Transfer to a rack and cool for 5 to 10 minutes. The shortcakes are best when served just baked and still warm. If you must bake them a few hours ahead, do not reheat; serve them at room temperature.

8. To assemble and serve, whip 1 cup of heavy cream with the vanilla until stiff.

9. Split the shortcakes horizontally, placing the bottoms on serving plates. Pour the remaining cup of cream over the biscuits and top with the berries. Sweeten the berries to taste by sifting confectioners' sugar over them. Add a dollop of whipped cream, cover with the remaining shortcake halves, and garnish with whipped cream.

SERVES 6 TO 8

Note: Johnnycake meal may be purchased by mail from Gray's Grist Mill Inc., P.O. Box 422, Adamsville, RI 02801; Telephone: (508) 636-6075. You may substitute the yellow or white cornmeal available at any supermarket, but the Gray's johnnycake meal is without question a superior product.

VARIATION: You can also serve these shortcake biscuits with fresh red raspberries, blackberries, or blueberries, alone or in combination.

Use the same quantity of berries; however, you may want to puree, sweeten, and strain a small portion of them as they do not have the juiciness of strawberries.

BAKED STUFFED-APPLE GRATIN

6 nonmealy apples: McIntosh, Cortland, or Macoun
1 cup Almond Paste (about 9 ounces) (page 207)
3 cups Mascarpone Custard (page 190)
2 tablespoons confectioners' sugar

1. Preheat the oven to 375 degrees.

2. Wash and core the apples. With a vegetable peeler remove about a 1-inch strip of the peel from the top of the apples.

3. With your fingers or the back of a spoon, push the almond paste into the cavities of the apples. Top with an extra tablespoon of the almond paste, covering the peeled surfaces with it.

4. Place the apples in a baking dish just large enough to accommodate them in one layer. Bake the apples until they are soft but not mushy, about 30 to 35 minutes. You should be able to pierce them easily with a cake tester or skewer. Check the apples after 20 minutes; if the almond paste has browned, cover the apples loosely with foil for the remainder of the baking time.

5. Remove the apples from the oven and increase the temperature to 500 degrees.

6. Pour the Mascarpone Custard over and around the apples and dust them with the confectioners' sugar. Bake them for 6 to 8 minutes, until the custard is heated through. Remove from the oven and change the oven setting to broil, placing the rack 4 to 5 inches below the heat source.

7. Brown the apples and custard under the broiler for 1 to 3 minutes, watching carefully to make sure the custard doesn't burn. Serve immediately.

SERVES 6

CANNOLI CREAM WITH FRESH BERRIES

This dessert cream was inspired by the filling for cannoli, the deep-fried Italian pastry. It is very easy to make and very elegant.

11 ounces ricotta (1 1/4 cups)
1/3 cup orange marmalade
2 ounces semisweet chocolate, chopped
1 tablespoon Grand Marnier
1/4 teaspoon pure vanilla extract
2 pints fresh raspberries, strawberries, or blueberries

1. Process the ricotta in a food processor, scraping down the sides of the bowl from time to time, for about 2 minutes, until the curds disappear and it is perfectly smooth.

2. Add the marmalade and pulse just to combine; you want to retain some small pieces of pulp.

3. Transfer to a mixing bowl. Fold in the chocolate, Grand Marnier, and vanilla. Refrigerate for at least 1 hour, or up to 2 days.

4. Divide the berries among 4 individual serving bowls or wine goblets. Pour the cannoli cream over the berries and serve.

SERVES 4 TO 6

ICE CREAM

When we opened Al Forno in our new location in July 1989, we decided to expand the dessert menu by adding ice cream and granita. Richard Sax, our dear friend, commented that we had truly gone off the deep end when we explained that our idea was to make them to order. Undaunted, we bought a dozen small machines, and every night we churn away.

There is really nothing like the taste of ice cream that comes right off the paddle just after being made. We think it is worth the effort in the restaurant and urge you to do it at home.

AL FORNO'S CINNAMON ICE CREAM

2 cups heavy cream
1 cup milk
2/3 cup sugar
4 cinnamon sticks
8 espresso or French-roast coffee beans

1. Combine all the ingredients in a saucepan. Scald over medium-high heat, stirring often, until the sugar dissolves. Set aside, uncovered, for 1 hour to steep.

2. Strain, chill, and freeze in an ice-cream maker according to the manufacturer's instructions.

MAKES ABOUT 3 CUPS

STRAWBERRY ICE CREAM
SCENTED WITH FRESH BASIL

2 cups heavy cream
1 cup milk
2/3 cup sugar
3/4 cup fresh basil leaves (see note)
1 pint strawberries, hulled, pureed, and strained
2 tablespoons Meyer's *liqueur de fraise* (optional)

1. Scald the cream, milk, sugar, and basil in a heavy saucepan, stirring to dissolve the sugar. Remove from the heat and set aside for 1 hour, uncovered, to steep.

2. Strain into a bowl, discarding the basil leaves. Fold in the strawberry puree and liqueur and chill for at least 1 hour.

3. Freeze in an ice-cream maker according to the manufacturer's instructions.

MAKES 1 QUART

Note: The basil adds a subtle, interesting flavor to this ice cream. If it is not available, do not be deterred from trying this recipe, as it will stand on its own without the herb.

FRESH CHERRY-VANILLA ICE CREAM

2 cups (6 ounces) Bing cherries, pitted and halved
4 tablespoons almond syrup (see note)
6 egg yolks
1/2 cup sugar
1 vanilla bean
2 cups heavy cream
2 cups milk

1. Combine the cherries and almond syrup in a small bowl; set aside in the refrigerator to marinate for about 1 hour.

2. Whisk the egg yolks and sugar together in a bowl.

3. Split the vanilla bean lengthwise with a paring knife and scrape the tiny black seeds from the pod. Combine the seeds, pod, cream, and milk in a heavy saucepan and scald over medium heat.

4. Very slowly, pour the hot cream into the egg yolks, whisking constantly. Return to the saucepan and cook over low heat, stirring with a wooden spoon until the mixture thickens enough to coat the back of the spoon, 5 to 10 minutes. Strain the custard into a bowl, discarding the vanilla pod, and chill for at least 2 hours.

5. Add the cherries and almond syrup to the chilled custard and freeze in an ice-cream maker according to the manufacturer's instructions.

MAKES A GENEROUS QUART

Note: Almond syrup is imported from Italy and France. It is available at specialty shops where it may be called *orzata* or *orgeat*.

Fresh Mint Ice Cream

2 cups fresh mint leaves, washed and patted dry
2 cups milk
2 cups heavy cream
6 egg yolks
1/2 cup sugar

1. Combine the mint, milk, and cream in a heavy saucepan and scald over medium heat. Remove from the heat and set aside, uncovered, for 1 hour, allowing the mint to infuse the cream.

2. Whisk the egg yolks and sugar together in a bowl.

3. Strain the cream, discarding the mint, and reheat to scalding.

4. Very slowly, add the hot cream to the yolks, whisking constantly. Return to the saucepan and cook over low heat, stirring with a wooden spoon, until the mixture thickens and coats the back of the spoon, 5 to 10 minutes.

5. Strain the custard into a bowl, chill, and freeze in an ice-cream maker according to the manufacturer's instructions.

MAKES A GENEROUS QUART

VARIATION: For Mint Chocolate-Chip Ice Cream, add 4 ounces of chopped semisweet chocolate halfway through the freezing process.

TARTUFO ICE CREAM

When a close family friend heard that I was going to Rome after graduating from RISD, she told me not to miss the *tartufo* at Tre Scalini, a lovely café in the Piazza Navona. It seemed strange that an ice cream would be made from truffles, but trusting the sophistication and taste of my friend, I ordered the tartufo. I was served not truffle-flavored ice cream but a ball of dense, rich chocolate ice cream with big chunks of bittersweet chocolate throughout, covered with a mound of unsweetened whipped cream. It was a combination of tastes in perfect balance, rich but not too sweet. That combination inspired me.

When we opened Al Forno, we had no freezer so I developed a cake with the same qualities. Now that we have a freezer specifically for ice cream, we can finally offer our interpretation of this fantastic Roman dessert and we rarely serve the cake.

2½ cups milk
4 egg yolks
1/2 cup sugar
8 ounces unsweetened chocolate, chopped
8 ounces semisweet chocolate, chopped
5 tablespoons heavy cream

1. Scald the milk in a heavy saucepan.

2. Whisk the yolks and sugar together in a mixing bowl. Slowly add the hot milk, whisking constantly. Return the mixture to the saucepan and cook over a low flame, stirring, until the custard coats the back of a spoon, 5 to 10 minutes.

3. Melt the unsweetened chocolate and 4 ounces of semisweet chocolate in a bowl over simmering water.

4. Through a fine mesh strainer, very slowly add the hot custard to the melted chocolate, whisking continuously. When all the custard is incorporated, whisk in the cream. Chill well and freeze in an ice-cream maker according to the manufacturer's instructions.

5. About 5 minutes before the ice cream is ready, add the remaining 4 ounces of chopped semisweet chocolate and continue to churn to combine. Serve with stiffly beaten unsweetened whipped cream.

MAKES 1 QUART

COFFEE MALTED ICE CREAM

2 cups milk
2 cups heavy cream
1/3 cup Horlicks malted milk
3 tablespoons Café Dolce (page 211)
6 egg yolks
1/2 cup sugar

1. Whisk together the milk, cream, malted milk, and Café Dolce in a heavy saucepan. Scald over medium heat.

2. Whisk the egg yolks and sugar together in a mixing bowl.

3. Very slowly, add the hot cream mixture to the yolks, whisking constantly. Return to the saucepan and cook over low heat, stirring, until the mixture thickens enough to coat the back of a spoon, 5 to 10 minutes.

4. Strain the custard into a bowl, chill, and freeze in an ice-cream maker according to the manufacturer's instructions.

MAKES 1 QUART

PANNA COTTA

The last time we were in Florence we were so intrigued by the snow-white appearance and pure flavor of *panna cotta* (cooked cream) that we tasted it every chance we got. The most interesting version was at Peppolino, a simple restaurant near Fiesole with a very imaginative menu. It is owned by a most welcoming husband-and-wife team. They served their *panna cotta* on a puree of fresh dates, elevating this simple dessert to grand proportions.

This is the *panna cotta* we serve at Al Forno. We do not often find fresh dates in Providence, so we serve this dessert accompanied by bitter chocolate sauce.

For variation, we infuse the cream with coffee beans or fresh mint.

1 package unflavored gelatin
4 tablespoons milk
2¼ cups heavy cream
1/2 cup confectioners' sugar
1/4 teaspoon pure vanilla extract

1. Butter 6 small custard cups or individual soufflé molds.

2. In a small bowl, soften the gelatin in the milk for about 10 minutes.

3. Combine the heavy cream and confectioners' sugar in a saucepan. Bring the cream to a boil, stirring to dissolve the sugar.

4. Remove the saucepan from the heat and add the vanilla and softened gelatin. Blend thoroughly. If the gelatin does not completely dissolve, return the saucepan to the stovetop and stir over very low heat until the gelatin particles disappear.

5. Pour the mixture into the molds and chill for about 2 hours, until the *panna cotta* are set.

6. To unmold, dip the molds in hot water for a moment and turn the *panna cotta* out onto individual plates. Serve with Bitter Chocolate Sauce (page 212), Caramel Sauce (page 213), or Coffee Crème Anglaise (page 210).

SERVES 6

Left to right: Rhode Island Shortcakes with Fresh Strawberries (page 194); Mom's Ricotta Balls (page 206); and Red-Raspberry Gratin (page 191).

MOM'S RICOTTA BALLS

These fritters are a specialty of George's mother, who has been making them for so long she no longer remembers the origin of the recipe. We fry the ricotta balls to order and serve them for dessert as part of our grand cookie finale.

1 pound ricotta
4 eggs
1 cup unbleached flour
3 teaspoons baking powder
1/8 teaspoon salt
Oil for deep frying
Confectioners' sugar for dusting

1. Whisk the ricotta and eggs together in a bowl.

2. Sift the flour with the baking powder and salt, and gently fold into the ricotta mixture.

3. Heat the oil to 375 degrees.

4. Drop rounded teaspoons of the batter into the hot oil and fry for about 2½ minutes per side, until golden brown. Drain on paper towels, transfer to a serving plate, and dust liberally with confectioners' sugar.

MAKES 50 TO 60 RICOTTA BALLS

ALMOND PASTE

lmond paste is available at most gourmet food stores and well-stocked supermarkets. It is also a snap to make. We use almond paste in the Baked Stuffed-Apple Gratin (page 196). It is also a great addition to bread pudding or in a fruit crostata.

2 cups whole blanched almonds
1/2 cup sugar
1 egg white
1/4 cup almond syrup (see note on page 200)

1. Combine the almonds and sugar in the bowl of a food processor fitted with a steel blade. Process until the nuts are ground fine and form a smooth paste.

2. Add the egg white and almond syrup. Process until well blended and smooth, scraping the bowl at least once. Store covered in the refrigerator until ready to use or overnight.

MAKES 1¾ TO 2 CUPS

CREAMY BREAD PUDDING

1 vanilla bean
6 cups heavy cream
8 eggs
1½ cups sugar
10 slices country bread, 3/8 inch thick, crusts removed

1. Split the vanilla bean in half lengthwise with a paring knife. Scrape the seeds from the pod and combine them with the pod and cream in a heavy saucepan.

2. Scald the cream, remove from the heat, and set aside, uncovered, for 1 hour to steep.

3. Preheat the oven to 300 degrees.

4. Strain the cream, discarding the pod, and reheat to scalding.

5. Whisk the eggs with the sugar in a mixing bowl. Very slowly, add the hot cream to the yolks, whisking constantly.

6. Arrange the bread slices in a 3-quart soufflé dish, overlapping the slices if necessary. Pour the custard mixture over the bread, submerging the slices with a spoon so they soak up some of the liquid.

7. Place the soufflé dish in a roasting pan, and fill the pan with enough hot water to come halfway up the side of the soufflé dish. Bake the pudding in its water bath for 30 to 40 minutes, until the edges have set and the center is still a bit runny. The pudding will continue to cook out of the oven and will set completely as it cools. For a smooth, creamy texture, stir the pudding every 5 minutes during baking: Run a rubber scraper around the inside of the soufflé dish, gently pushing the outside of the pudding toward the center. The pudding will cook evenly, and the custard will be silky-smooth. Serve the bread pudding warm.

SERVES 10 TO 12

VARIATION: For a lovely autumn bread pudding, follow the above directions, adding 2 teaspoons of fennel seeds to the cream and vanilla in step 1. Proceed with steps 2 through 4, discarding the fennel seeds with the vanilla pod in step 4. Continue with step 5, reducing the sugar beaten into the eggs to 3/4 cup. After completing step 6, top the pudding with 1 cup of seedless grapes and 3 cored and thinly sliced Empire apples. Just before baking (step 7), drizzle the top with 3 tablespoons melted butter and proceed with the rest of the recipe. The pigment in the skin of the Empire apple lends a lovely pink hue to the flesh of the fruit. You may substitute another type of apple in this recipe, but the Empires make a lovely presentation.

NANCI COURTNEY'S CRÈME ANGLAISE

Nanci Courtney is an alumna of the Al Forno kitchen. She is a great cook, with a real gift for desserts. Here is her crème anglaise.

2 cups heavy cream
4 egg yolks
1/4 cup sugar
1/2 teaspoon pure vanilla extract

1. Scald the cream in a heavy saucepan.

2. Whisk the egg yolks and sugar together until blended. Add the hot cream in a slow steady stream, whisking constantly. When all the cream has been incorporated, pour the mixture into a clean saucepan.

3. Cook the crème anglaise over medium heat, stirring constantly, until the mixture thickens and coats a spoon. *Do not allow it to boil.*

4. Immediately pour the custard through a fine strainer into a mixing bowl set over a bowl of ice. Stir the custard over ice for several minutes to cool. Add the vanilla and stir to combine. Refrigerate until ready to use, or up to 2 days.

MAKES 2½ TO 3 CUPS

VARIATION: For Coffee Crème Anglaise, follow this recipe and add 2 to 3 tablespoons of Café Dolce (page 211).

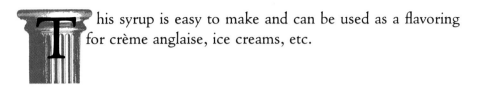

This syrup is easy to make and can be used as a flavoring for crème anglaise, ice creams, etc.

2 cups strong espresso
5 tablespoons superfine sugar

Combine the espresso and sugar in a heavy saucepan. Bring to a boil, lower the heat, and simmer until the liquid is reduced to 1/2 cup. Cool to room temperature and then cover and refrigerate for up to 2 weeks.

MAKES 1/2 CUP

BITTER CHOCOLATE SAUCE

We use this sauce with our Panna Cotta (page 204). It is also great over ice cream for sundaes.

1/2 cup unsweetened cocoa powder
1 teaspoon potato flour
2 tablespoons sugar
3 cups heavy cream

1. Combine the cocoa, potato flour, sugar, and 2 cups of heavy cream in a saucepan. Bring to a boil, whisking out any lumps. Lower the heat and simmer, stirring, for 3 to 4 minutes to cook out the taste of the flour.

2. Slowly whisk in the remaining cream. If you find the sauce too thick, you can whisk in up to 1 cup more cream. Serve warm or chilled. It will keep, refrigerated, for 2 days.

MAKES 3½ CUPS

CARAMEL SAUCE

This dessert sauce is very versatile. It is good with Panna Cotta (page 204), as an ice-cream topping, or drizzled over Caramelized Pumpkin Crostata (page 188).

2 cups heavy cream
1/2 cup sugar

1. Scald the cream, reduce the heat to very low, and keep warm.

2. Heat the sugar in a heavy saucepan over medium heat, stirring often with a wooden spoon. Do not use a metal spoon, as the high heat produced by the sugar will be conducted through the spoon, making it too hot to hold. The sugar will slowly melt into a clear liquid and gradually darken. Don't worry if the sugar lumps. Break up the lumps with the wooden spoon, and they will melt into the caramel as it darkens.

3. When the caramel has turned a rich mahogany color, pour it slowly into the hot cream, whisking constantly. The caramel will spatter so be careful not to burn yourself. If the temperature of the cream is too low, you may find that portions of the caramel solidify in it. In that case, increase the flame under the cream and stir until the bits melt and the mixture becomes smooth. The caramel sauce thickens as it cools and will solidify in the refrigerator, where it will keep for up to 2 days. It may be reheated gently to pouring consistency.

MAKES 2 CUPS

INDEX